LYME DISEASE

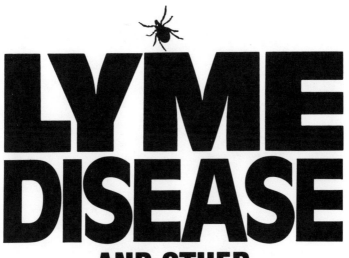

LYME DISEASE

AND OTHER PEST-BORNE ILLNESSES
BY SEAN P. MACTIRE

FRANKLIN WATTS
NEW YORK   LONDON   TORONTO   SYDNEY
A VENTURE BOOK

Photographs copyright ©: Centers for Disease Control: pp. 14, 23, 41, 45; Gamma-Liaison: pp. 16 (Stephen Castagneto), 58 (D. Sorine); Photo Researchers, Inc.: pp. 29 (Charles R. Belinky), 50, 55, 62 (all Hank Morgan/ Science Source), 53 (Johannes Hofmann/Okapia); John F. Anderson: p. 31 (originally printed in *The Yale Journal*, 57, 1984); Animals Animals: p. 57 (Roger & Donna Aitkenhead); The Bettmann Archive: p. 67.

Library of Congress Cataloging-in-Publication Data

Mactire, Sean P.
Lyme disease and other pest-borne illnesses / by Sean P. Mactire
p.   cm.   — (A Venture book)
Includes bibliographical references and index.
Summary: Describes the causes, symptoms, and treatment of Lyme
disease and examines other pest-borne diseases.
ISBN 0-531-12523-8
1. Lyme disease.   2. Zoonoses.   [1. Lyme disease.   2. Animals as
carriers of disease.]   I. Title
(RC155.5.M33   1992
616.9'2—dc20   91-40895 CIP AC

Contents

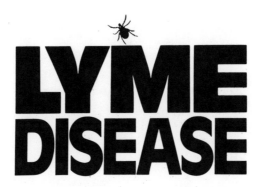

LYME DISEASE

Introduction

Most people think of ticks and fleas as nasty pests that make their lovable cats and dogs miserable and sick. The last thing that comes to mind is the possibility of illness and disease in humans. Yet this possibility is the primary reason we now have for trying to protect our cats and dogs from becoming infested with these insects. We tend not to think of how harmful fleas and ticks can be to people since we are not as helpless as our pets. But these bugs can create serious hazards for us as well. Ticks alone carry over half a dozen diseases, one of which—Lyme disease—has reached epidemic proportions in the United States.

Much of this book will explore the most newly discovered tick-borne illness—Lyme disease—and how to protect yourself against it. Most of the older diseases have been kept at bay, at least temporarily, by the medical advances of the twentieth century. This is precisely why most people do not associate fleas, ticks, and lice with disease that can afflict and even kill them. Few people in the 1990s are old enough to remember the millions of people massacred by pest-borne diseases in the 1890s and the early 1900s.

Lyme disease is the first national pest-borne epidemic of the late twentieth century (post–World War II). It is only through this frightening new scourge that the public has become aware of the danger of ticks, but fleas and lice are just as dangerous to humans, if not more so. Most animals infected by pest-borne disease do not become as seriously ill as humans.

In this book, you will discover the history of these diseases, how they're transmitted, how to avoid infection, and how to control the spread of pest-borne diseases. You will find out where the diseases are most likely to occur, how to detect the leading symptoms, and when and how to get treatment. You will also find out how to avoid the danger of misdiagnosis by learning to spot these diseases and knowing how they affect you once they are contracted.

First, we'll look at Lyme disease: What it is and how to protect ourselves against it.

1 What Is Lyme Disease?

Lyme disease was named for the place in which it first appeared in the United States—Lyme, Connecticut. It is transmitted to people when a diseased tick decides to find a meal and bites a human instead of an animal. The illness is caused by a spirochete of the Borrelia family, and, unfortunately, usually goes unrecognized at first by the person who's been bitten by the tick. The disease is usually contracted between June and September when the tick is most active and many people are spending a lot of their time outdoors.

The disease first came to light in Lyme, Connecticut, in October 1975. Several patients at that time had reported fatigue, pain, and a rash on their hands to their doctors, who, in turn, reported these symptoms to the Connecticut State Health Department. Most of the cases involved children who also complained of arthritislike symptoms. At first, it was thought that the illness was a previously unrecognized disease, and because of these quite ordinary symptoms it was called "Lyme arthritis." But when the Connecticut State

Health Department received phone calls from *two* mothers whose children had been diagnosed as having juvenile rheumatoid arthritis, a research team headed by Dr. Allen C. Steere, a postgraduate fellow in rheumatology at the Yale University Medical School, went to Lyme to investigate.

A surprise was in store for Dr. Steere and his colleagues: Thirty-nine children in this small rural community of Lyme, Connecticut, had been diagnosed as having developed juvenile rheumatoid arthritis. It was incredible to the researchers that a noncommunicable disease such as arthritis could have affected so many children in such a small area; normally there should have been not more than one case in a population of that size. The mystified investigators decided that the situation needed thorough study. Rheumatoid arthritis, when it strikes children, is a crippling illness that blights their entire future; the suffering and debilitation lasts a lifetime. With this prognosis dooming their children's futures, it's no wonder their parents were looking for more answers and were unwilling to settle for the initial diagnosis. In addition, there were twelve adults who had been newly diagnosed as having an inflammatory arthritis. At this point, health officials determined that these abnormal findings had to be more than merely a regional phenomenon. Maybe some environmental poison was to blame, or possibly the beginning of a major epidemic had occurred. To add to the mystery, the cases had an unusual pattern—most of the victims lived in heavily wooded areas.

To Dr. Steere and his investigative team, the facts indicated that this disease was clearly no ordinary form of rheumatoid arthritis. Although there were few clues as to its cause, Dr. Steere quickly made several important findings.

One discovery was that the disease was not particularly contagious; individuals in the same family often contracted it in different years. Another finding was that the majority of these cases, regardless of the year, first developed symptoms during the summer months. A third finding was that 25 percent of the patients interviewed remembered having a strange skin rash from one to several weeks before the onset of the arthritislike pains. The descriptions of the rashes were remarkably similar. They all had started out as a small red papule, or bump, and gradually expanded to form a bull's-eye shape from 4 to 20 inches (10 to 50 cm) in diameter. The occurrence of the rash on the back, chest, or buttocks of most patients suggested that a crawling insect, rather than a flying insect, had transmitted the disease. Yet none of the victims could remember having been bitten by one.

Dr. Steere concluded, on the basis of these findings, that he was dealing with a previously unrecognized disease probably caused by a virus and transmitted by an unknown arthropod (the group to which insects, spiders, and ticks belong). He was the one who named it Lyme disease or Lyme arthritis for the town in which it was first observed.

In 1975 and 1976, he began testing blood taken from the victims of Lyme disease for the presence of specific antibodies of thirty-eight known tick-borne diseases and 178 other arthropod-transmitted viruses. Antibodies are formed as a result of exposure to disease bacteria and viruses. Not a single test result was positive, indicating that none of the known diseases had caused this illness. As he continued to carry out his research, Dr. Steere finally came across some intriguing information: In 1977, nine of the patients affected by the rash that year remembered having been bitten by a tick at the site of the rash. One of them had actually removed the tick, saved it, and gave it to Dr. Steere for identification. The tick, barely larger than a

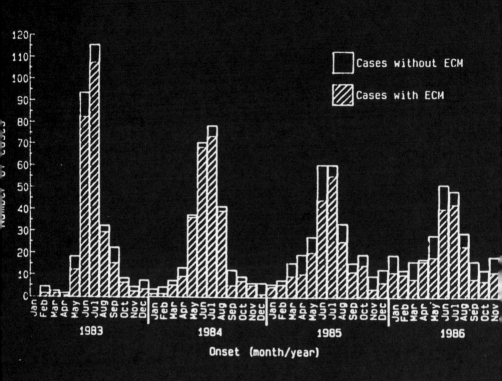

Lyme disease cases, by month and year of onset, United States, 1983–1986

Cases without ECM
Cases with ECM

Onset (month/year)

This chart shows that not only are most cases of Lyme disease marked by the ECM rash, but that more cases occur in June and July than during any other month.

pinhead, was a dark brown, hard-bodied insect that might easily have been mistaken for a piece of dirt had it not bitten a human. It was hardly surprising that it had taken Dr. Steere and his team almost two years to determine that the tick was the probable culprit, in view of its size. The tick was identified by Andrew Spielman of the Harvard School of Public Health as *Ixodes dammini*, a species closely related to *I. ricinus*, the tick responsible for the European version of Lyme disease: erythema chronicum migrans disease (ECM).

Erythema chronicum migrans (ECM) literally means "chronic migrating red rash," and it was discovered in Europe in 1909. ECM usually appears as a growing lesion often accompanied by central clearing, such as the bull's-eye mark that was noticed in Lyme disease. This lesion is the hallmark of the disease. ECM can disappear after about four weeks when it's known more simply as EMD (erythema migrans disease), or it can exist in its chronic form and be accompanied by symptoms such as headache, sore throat, fever and/or fatigue, arthritis or arthralgia, impairment of the brain and nervous system, and probable cardiac involvement.

Once the *I. dammini* tick had been identified as the vector, or carrier, of Lyme disease, investigators hoped to next isolate the actual agent of infection. First they needed to be absolutely certain that the tick was indeed the carrier of Lyme disease. If the distribution of the *I. dammini* tick in the wild corresponded to the pattern of the outbreak of Lyme disease, the circumstantial evidence would point to this particular bug. Still, the agent or cause of both ECM and Lyme disease remained elusive. Repeated cell cultures and microscopic investigation of the tick's internal organs failed to reveal the presence of a bacterium or any other pathogen (cause of disease).

Then the break finally came.

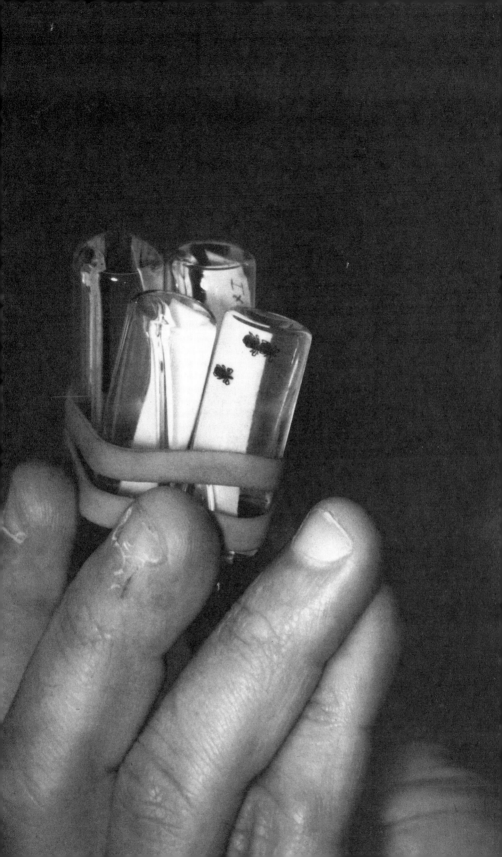

In the fall of 1981, a fatal case of Rocky Mountain spotted fever, a rickettsia disease transmitted by the dog tick, was reported on Shelter Island, off the coast of eastern Long Island. The New York State Department of Health sent a team of biologists there to collect live ticks. Because the normal vector tick for Rocky Mountain spotted fever, *Dermacentor variabilis*, is not found in the fall, adult *Ixodes dammini* ticks were collected instead. They were sent to the Rocky Mountain Laboratories in Hamilton, Montana, for study.

There, Willy Burgdorfer, an international authority on tick-borne diseases, examined the digestive tract of the Ixodes tick with dark-field microscopy. To his astonishment, he found the innards teeming not with the rickettsiae that cause Rocky Mountain spotted fever, but with long, irregularly shaped spirochete bacteria. Burgdorfer knew that *I. dammini* had been implicated as the probable vector for Lyme disease, and he knew that spirochetes were not the infectious agent in Rocky Mountain spotted fever. He wondered whether he had just discovered the bacteria that was the cause of Lyme disease. Fortunately, another researcher at the Rocky Mountain Laboratory, Alan D. Barbour, was able to grow the spirochetes in pure culture and obtain sufficient quantities for further experimentation.

By the summer of 1982, spirochetes had been isolated from the blood, skin, and cerebrospinal fluid of Lyme disease victims by investigators at the New

Compare the size of these deer ticks to that of the fingers holding the tubes to see how small the ticks really are.

17

York State Department of Health and at Yale University Medical School. Russell C. Johnson and his colleagues at the University of Minnesota Medical School studied the Lyme disease spirochete. They determined, on the basis of its DNA structure, that it was an entirely new species in the genus *Borrelia*. So, in 1984, Burgdorfer received the dubious honor of having the new spirochete named after him. Henceforth it would be known as *Borrelia burgdorferi*.

Once *B. burgdorferi* had been conclusively identified as the agent of Lyme disease, it was then possible to track its distribution in nature. Edward M. Bosler of the New York State Department of Health found the spirochete in the tissues of several mammals, including field mice, voles, and deer, as well as in all of the developmental stages of the *I. dammini* tick. With the last puzzle piece in place, correlations could now be drawn between Lyme disease and the tick-borne diseases discovered in the early 1900s in Europe.

Every decade of this century has seen a new piece added to the patchwork of knowledge about these diseases. First, the Swedish dermatologist Afzelius isolated erythema migrans; then researchers in Austria discovered its possibly chronic nature, and it was renamed erythema *chronicum* migrans (ECM). In France in 1922, bacterial meningitis was first related to tick-borne disease. Bacterial meningitis is characterized by a rapidly progressive feverish illness that leads to delirium, coma, and convulsions. In 1934 the symptoms were even more well defined in Germany, and in the 1940s polio was also listed as one of the illnesses from this tick-borne disease.

In the 1950s, penicillin was discovered to be effective as a treatment for both ECM and tick-borne meningitis. In the 1960s and 1970s, erythema migrans disease (EMD) became the clinical foundation for all of the subsequent discoveries relating to Lyme disease. It was also discovered that EMD can be transmitted from human to human. The history of EMD and ECM shows how tick-borne diseases have spread throughout Europe and also demonstrates the benefits of using antibiotics in treating Lyme disease.

Earlier, it was believed that ECM was the result of an allergic reaction to a toxin in the tick, but the effectiveness of treatment with penicillin proved that ECM was a true disease. Spirochetes actually became the prime suspects as early as 1948. Those suspicions were proven in 1962 in connection with typhus, which can also be transmitted by ticks.

When the first case of ECM was described in the United States in 1970, some investigators actually believed that the illness was caused by an infectious nonbacterial but antibiotic sensitive agent. Possibly this kind of thinking was due to the fact that the spirochete that causes Lyme disease was so elusive that it was not found until several years after the outbreak in Lyme, when Burgdorfer examined the *I. dammini* tick with dark-field microscopy.

Dr. Burgdorfer and Dr. Steere and his team concluded from their investigations that Lyme disease was a totally new form of ECM. This discovery was fortunate because the realization that ECM and Lyme disease were separate expressions of the same agent meant that Lyme disease could be treated as long as it could be properly diagnosed. These investigations also resulted in the alarming conclusion that Lyme disease was definitely *not* just a localized phenomenon threatening the residents of Lyme, Connecticut, and environs. Because of the large number of animals that could be carriers for the spirochete, it could appear anywhere. In fact, the same spirochete was isolated and identified in ticks in California as well.

THE RANGE OF THE DISEASE

What began as a local curiosity has grown into a national and worldwide nightmare. Lyme disease has been reported in forty-six U.S. states and on five continents. The Centers for Disease Control in Atlanta, Georgia, considers Lyme disease to be the most important tick-borne disease in the United States. The total number of its U.S. victims is unknown, but all the experts agree that the roughly 5,000 new cases reported in 1988 were but a fraction of the true count because the disease can imitate so many other conditions. With several thousand people infected each year, the incidence of Lyme disease now surpasses that of Rocky Mountain spotted fever, which, before 1981, had been the most prevalent and well-known tick-borne disease.

The Centers for Disease Control reports that Lyme disease has spread to forty-six states, with the majority of the cases still occurring in nine states: California, Connecticut, Massachusetts, Maryland, Minnesota, New Jersey, New York, Rhode Island, and Wisconsin. Located in all these states are "endemic" areas for Lyme disease, which means that the disease is commonly found in that area. These high-risk areas are southeast and coastal Connecticut; Cape Cod and the nearby islands of Nantucket and Martha's Vineyard, Massachusetts and Block Island, Rhode Island; New York's Long Island and Westchester and Putnam counties; central and southern New Jersey; west-central and northwest Wisconsin; east-central Minnesota; and the coastal counties of California north of San Francisco.

Outside the United States, Lyme disease and ECM have been recognized in nineteen countries, including Australia. In Europe the culprit is *Ixodes ricinus*, which is widely distributed from the coastal areas of Scandinavia to the northern parts of Spain and Italy. Mosquitoes have been reported as the vector in Sweden, as well as in Australia, where other insects have also been implicated. This discovery suggests that any insect that attacks host animals—which includes birds—can become infected and thus carry the disease to humans. It's a distinct probability, therefore, that, with the help of migratory birds, in the future the disease could spread worldwide.

2 Pests and Disease

There are several varieties of ticks in the world, but not all carry the Lyme spirochete. The ticks involved in the spread of Lyme disease belong to the genus *Ixodes*. *Ixodes* ticks are notorious vectors of disease: European *I. ricinus* has been implicated as the carrier of at least eight diverse veterinary infections; Eurasian *I. persulcatus* transmits four diseases; and the American *I. dammini* transmits both a rodent disease and the Lyme disease spirochete.

There are two kinds of ticks, which differ considerably in habits and appearance and are easily distinguished. The *Ixodes*, or "hard ticks," are characterized by a hard plate or shield on the anterior region of the back. This shield covers the entire back of the male but only a small portion of the back of the female, whose body is capable of great distention after feeding. The mouthparts of hard ticks are visible from above as they project in front of the body. The *Argasidae*, or "soft ticks," have no dorsal plate, and the outer surface is rough and thrown into numerous creases and folds. Their mouthparts are under the body and are not visible from above.

Ixodes dammini *ticks at different stages of development*

THE LIFE CYCLE OF *IXODES*

The female *Ixodes* tick is most usually noticed, since it stays attached to the animal or person it attacks for a long period of time and swells up to the size of a green pea. After the female has taken a meal of blood, it drops off to the ground and, after a period of several weeks, it proceeds to lay eggs. The eggs are laid at the roots of grass and among plant debris. Each of the eggs is covered with a viscid secretion which prevents it from drying out. Larvae with three pairs of legs hatch from the eggs. After a resting period, the larvae climb up to the tips of blades of grass or other plants, and wait for a host to feed on. Ticks can neither hop nor fly (they have no wings), and their legs are not very efficient. So they wait until a host comes near enough for them to drop or crawl onto. When they succeed in finding a suitable host, they select a comfortable spot and embed their mouthparts in the skin. They remain attached for three to four days while taking a blood meal, and then drop off to the ground. Here the larvae retire to chinks and crevices and molt to the next stage, which is that of an eight-legged nymph. The nymph climbs up grass or plants and seeks another host in the same way as the larvae did. It remains attached for about five days and then drops to the ground to molt to the adult stage. The adults repeat the process, but only the females take a prolonged meal of blood, which lasts from eight to nine days. The males may attach lightly for a few hours, but their main concern is to find and mate with the females. Thus, there are several periods in a tick's lifetime when the tick is dangerous to animals and humans.

Like other ticks, *Ixodes* are able to survive long periods of starvation, which is essential for their continued survival in view of their uncertain chance of reaching a host. Larvae have been found to be able to feed after fifteen months' starvation, and nymphs, after a period of thirteen months. Unfed adults have survived for twenty-one months. The opportunity of feeding regulates the speed of development, since a tick cannot evolve to its next stage of development without feeding. Development is also dependent on the temperature. Winter is too cold for feeding, and, of course, fewer hosts are available in winter. In spring and autumn, the ticks make periodic attempts to feed. During the summer months development proceeds, but there is little feeding.

Ixodes are also very sensitive to dry air and cannot be reared in the laboratory at humidities below 80 percent. In nature, the greatest danger of water loss occurs when ticks are seeking hosts at the tips of grass and foliage, and they never attempt this in extremely hot weather.

FLEAS

In the study of Lyme disease, it is also important to know about fleas since fleas are carriers of major diseases and will likely become carriers of Lyme disease in the near future.

Fleas constitute about a thousand species worldwide. All fleas are, in their adult form, parasitic on warm-blooded animals. The body of the flea is compressed laterally; it is "streamlined" and covered with backward-directed bristles. These modifications contribute tremendously to the flea's ability to move easily through fur or feathers on the host's body. Fleas are also extraordinarily good jumpers, which means they can infest an area more easily than ticks can. They deposit their eggs on floor cracks, on carpets, and in upholstered furniture.

There are seven common kinds of fleas: *Pulex, Ctenocephalides, Ceratophyllus, Nosopsyllus, Spilop-*

syllus, *Letopsyllus*, and *Xenopsyllus*. The genus *Ctenocephalides* includes the cat and dog fleas, *C. felis* and *C. canis*.

Fleas can live for several months, but only spend a small portion of that time on the host from which they feed. Aside from transmitting disease, flea bites result in intense itching and severe infections, which can lead to gangrene. They sometimes deposit eggs into wounds.

Keeping pets clean and using insecticides will help keep fleas at bay. In cases of severe infestation, allergies may result from the breathing in of body sheddings of fleas and ticks, but more commonly from ticks. This kind of reaction is rare and is similar to a pollen reaction in its symptoms. The more common allergy is that caused by a tick bite, which is similar to a bee sting, and is treated by the removal of the tick.

Ticks and fleas are parasites that attack warm-blooded animals such as rodents, deer, cattle, sheep, horses, as well as dogs and cats. Sometimes the host animals themselves can infect humans, but more often humans are infected by the ticks and fleas that move from the animal to the human. Close contact with host animals allows this to happen.

LICE

Lice have been lousing up the lives of human beings ever since the dawn of time. There are three species of lice: the body louse (*Pediculus humanus humanus*), the head louse (*Pediculus humanus capitus*), and the pubic or crab louse (*Phthirus pubis*). Body lice transmit typhus, trench fever and louse-borne relapsing fever. The head and pubic louse are not known to transmit disease.

Head and body lice are nasty little pests (2 to 4 mm in length) that are similar in appearance. They are elongated and flat, have soft, tough skin and are dirty white to gray in color. Head lice only inhabit head hair around the nape of the neck and behind the ears. They are rarely seen on eyebrows and lashes.

Crab lice are circular and look like very tiny crabs. They infest the genital and rectal areas. They can infest upper body hair as well, including eyelashes, facial hair, and underarm hair, but rarely the head. They also feed on blood.

A female body louse lays up to 250 eggs in clothing or on body hairs. The eggs are oval and grayish white and cannot be removed by bathing. They hatch within a week and mature within eight to nine days. These are blood-sucking parasites that must feed or die. But they are susceptible to temperature changes. They live for about a month.

Head and body louse infestations are commonly associated with poverty, conditions of overcrowding, and bad sanitary environments. Infestation can be contracted from skin-to-skin contact, infested clothing and bedding, and from infested upholstered furniture. Crab louse infestations are usually sexually transmitted, but can be contracted from infested bedding, clothing, toilet seats, and bathtubs.

Louse powders were developed during World War II and usually contained DDT. When DDT was banned, it was replaced by dieldrin, lindane, or pyrethrins. Other products contain carbaryl or malathion. There are many products on the market to kill lice, and one should consult a physician if an infestation occurs.

A discussion of the variety of diseases carried by pests will be covered in Chapter Seven.

To reiterate, the primary guilt for spreading Lyme disease rests with the *Ixodes dammini* tick, commonly known as the deer tick. Most Lyme disease cases still occur in the Northeast, where the disease cycle is spread by three performers: the deer tick, the white-footed deer mouse, and the white-tailed deer. The mature tick feeds and mates on the deer, and then drops to the ground to lay eggs. When the eggs hatch into the larval stage they are infected with the Lyme disease spirochete by the deer mouse, which was always, in the Northeast area, the original carrier of the disease. Eventually the larvae molt into the nymph stage, which is a sort of adolescence for ticks. It's at this stage that the tick is most dangerous to humans and domestic animals.

I. dammini's life cycle seems to take approximately two years to complete. The adult tick feeds during the earlier part of winter; the larva feeds during the spring and in its greatest period of activity—early summer. This is also the time when people spend a large portion of their days outside. Nymphs are much, much smaller than adult ticks—about the size of the period at the end of this sentence—so they are not easy to find on skin or clothing. It is possible to have been bitten by a nymph tick and not even notice it. Seventy to 90 percent of the people who eventually contract Lyme disease are bitten by nymphs. Because they are so tiny, nymphs readily take a free ride to other localities by means of biting ground-feeding birds and hanging on until the bird has flown to a distant area. Rabbits are hosts to these parasites as well.

The white-tailed deer is probably the major inadvertent transporter of infected ticks to new areas. Some experts on Lyme disease believe that the epidemic started as a result of a burgeoning deer population. The nation's deer population has grown from about half a million at the beginning of this century to 15 million today. It's no longer necessary for people to go for hikes in the woods to be endangered by the ticks carrying Lyme disease; the ticks will inhabit their lawns and gardens and come into their homes on the fur of their

*The large deer population and lack of
wildland for them to roam has forced
them to live closer to the human population.*

household pets. The growth of the suburbs farther and farther from our cities has destroyed much of the deer's formerly wild habitat. Deer are now commonly seen grazing in residential lawns and gardens. The people in the greatest danger from Lyme disease, experts believe, are those who can see deer from their homes.

Destroying the deer population is not the solution to stopping the spread of Lyme disease, although it has been suggested. Infected adult ticks become a more immediate threat when they are denied access to their more usual hosts such as deer.

The people who live on one Massachusetts island have reason to regret that its deer were almost all killed. Homeless ticks, in their search for new hosts, have become a menace to humans. Dogs and horses, which both have closer contact with people than deer do, can become crippled by Lyme disease as well as bring it closer to people.

In the western United States, *I. pacificus* is the tick that transmits Lyme disease to human hosts. Nymphs of both tick species may attach themselves to a great assortment of animals. These include reptiles, birds, possums, rodents, rabbits, hooved animals such as cattle, sheep, and deer, and carnivores such as dogs and wolves.

There are indications that Lyme disease will soon be carried by fleas, spiders, and possibly even flies. At the minimum, twenty-nine species of mammals have been implicated as hosts, and thirty-eight species of birds have been discovered as carriers of Lyme disease.

A composite diagram (see page 31) shows the life stages of *I. dammini*, the relationship of this tick to its vertebrate hosts, and the tick's natural means of dispersal. Mammals and birds are either maintenance or incidental hosts. Maintenance hosts are animals, such

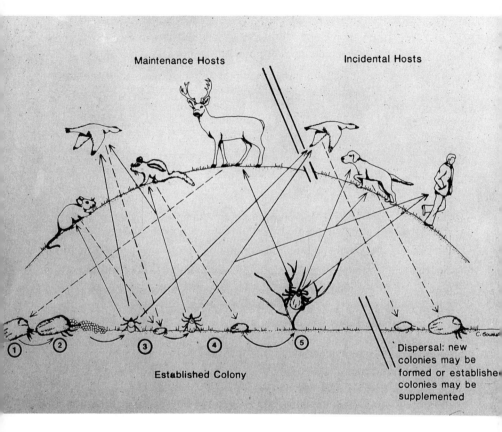

The life cycle of Ixodes dammini
Key: 1—engorged female;
2—adult female laying eggs;
3—questing and engorged larva;
4—questing and engorged nymph;
5—questing adult;
questing tick finds host;
tick feeds and drops from host;
tick develops to next stage.

as mice, birds, chipmunks, and white-tailed deer, that regularly and dependably serve as sources of blood for the mobile ticks near or in habitats suitable for the ticks' survival. Incidental hosts are those that chiefly serve to disperse the parasite (such as birds and transient hunting dogs) or those, such as humans, that are fed upon occasionally but, compared with other hosts, do not significantly enhance tick survival.

3 How Do You Get Lyme Disease?

Lyme disease is caused by the spirochete *B. burgdorferi*, a corkscrew-shaped bacteria, and is most commonly transmitted to humans in the bite of the deer tick. The tick injects spirochete-laden saliva into the blood stream or deposits fecal matter onto the skin. Once these spirochetes are injected under the skin by the tick, they incubate for three to thirty-two days and then migrate, which causes the characteristic bull's-eye skin lesion associated with ECM and Lyme disease. During their investigation of the cause of Lyme disease, the Yale investigators found out that while few patients were aware of having had a tick bite, they did recall that an unusual red skin rash had preceded their arthritis. About two-thirds of Lyme disease patients notice such a rash—the earliest sign of infection.

The following cases narrate the harrowing experiences of Lyme disease victims. The first shows how vitally important it is to be informed in order to prevent Lyme disease.

THE CITY DWELLER

D. was an urban professional who felt most at home with the rich variety and rapid pace of city life, and felt "out of it" when visiting the suburbs or the country. After finally yielding to her friends' insistence to visit them at their home on Shelter Island, she found herself in a discussion of Lyme disease with her hosts on Memorial Day weekend, 1985. At that time, little was known publicly about the disease or any prevention methods.

That Saturday night, D. and her friends went out for a walk with the dog through the adjacent woods. Because of their previous discussion, D. quickly checked herself for ticks before going to bed that night. Not realizing how small a tick could be and having never felt so much as a bite that evening, she retired, satisfied that she was free of ticks.

Days later, after she was back in the city, she noticed a rash. It did not appear to be severe, so D. did not, at that time, think it was important to get medical attention. She treated the rash with a nonprescription cream and went carefree about her business. The rash dutifully disappeared, but then soon afterward she started experiencing flu-like symptoms. She had muscle aches and headaches, plus a low-grade fever for over a week. Again, D. treated it herself with nonprescription cold medications and continued with her busy work schedule.

Weeks later, D. woke up agonized with pain. She tried to rest as much as possible, in spite of her physical distress, but within a day she had extreme difficulty walking. This compelled D. to finally see her doctor, who was familiar with Lyme disease. He had seen it in many patients who spent weekends in the outlying suburbs during the summer. His suspicions that D.

had Lyme disease grew as she informed him of the visit to her friends who lived near the woods and their hike, of the rash and the recent episode of the "flu."

Her first blood test proved negative for Lyme disease. However, her doctor decided to administer a course of antibiotics, which eliminated the first arthritis-like symptoms. A second test confirmed the presence of Lyme disease and D. is being treated with frequent antibiotic therapy. However, she still suffers from repeated attacks of arthritic symptoms. She keeps hoping for a cure. Had D. been better informed, and had she known how to prevent Lyme disease, her current suffering could have been avoided.

The second case shows how the symptoms of Lyme disease can mislead even the well-informed.

THE DOCTOR

This crisis began when T. was playing tennis with his friends in July, 1987. He became overwhelmed with exhaustion, and upon taking his pulse, he found it to be 150 beats per minute, more than twice as fast as an adult's normal rate.

His tennis partner, also a doctor, took charge of T. and took him to the local hospital, where it was determined that he had a heart block—a disorder that usually strikes elderly people who have atherosclerosis, not an active, younger man with no history of heart disease. Fortunately, T.'s friend was acquainted with Lyme disease. Knowing that a heart block in a younger person is one of its major symptoms, he asked T. about other symptoms. T. replied that he had noticed a rash on his thigh that morning. On inspection the rash appeared to T. and his colleagues to look like the classic Lyme disease rash seen on numerous victims.

In processing the history of his current illness, T. recalled that for six weeks he had been suffering with a stiff neck, which was now considered to be aseptic meningitis. T. was in the habit of taking a morning run, and for the past month, he had noticed an unusual lethargy during this activity. T. then abruptly realized that the place where he ran was infested with Lyme disease ticks. As in the case of most victims, T. had not noticed being bitten by a tick.

On the basis of this history, T. was immediately started on a course of antibiotics. However, he refused to be hospitalized, which, in view of how dangerously ill he was, he now feels was a wrong decision.

Soon, T. felt much better, which was not surprising since his blood tests showed the highest level of disease activity ever seen in the hospital. Over the next two months, his heart rhythm gradually returned to normal, and as he improved, the difference made T. realize how very ill he had been feeling in the weeks before his diagnosis.

One of the problems in detecting and treating Lyme disease is its changeability. Symptoms vary from one patient to another, and as is illustrated in this story, spotting the disease can be extraordinarily difficult. Living with it, however, can be a wretched ordeal.

THE SUBURBAN FAMILY

In 1983, the B. family moved into what they thought was a lovely home in the suburbs. Its location close to a wooded area would give, they felt, their three boys the opportunity to experience and learn from nature firsthand. They had not been informed by the realtor that

36

the area had a major Lyme disease problem, but they were confronted with it that summer when their eldest son developed the telltale rash. Mrs. B. had just read about a case of Lyme disease in the newspaper and took the boy to their doctor immediately. Her diagnosis was confirmed professionally and the course of treatment was successful.

The following summer, the family's four-year-old had great difficulty walking after waking up. One knee was stiff and swollen. In his case there was no rash, so the doctor missed the diagnosis completely. The boy's discomfort did not abate and the family changed physicians. At this time the boy developed an ear infection and the new doctor treated it with antibiotics. The medication also relieved the stiffness and swelling in his leg. Since then, he has had two more bouts every other summer. These subsequent episodes, however, have been accompanied by the appearance of a rash. Neither boy ever tested positive for Lyme disease, possibly because of the early treatment each child received.

In the summer of 1988, the youngest boy became ill. He became weak, tired quickly, and was very sensitive to being touched. Although the doctor did not suspect Lyme disease, he treated the boy with antibiotics, and the child improved. In this case and all the previous ones, none of the children remembered getting bitten by a tick.

Lyme disease has caused major changes in the way the family lives. The children are now only allowed to play near the house, and Mrs. B. has become a watchdog of sorts. She keeps a careful record of any symptoms her children develop. If any child is bitten by a tick, she removes it and carefully tapes it to an index card. Then she keeps a close eye on the child. She is aware of the tragedy of other cases—children with paralysis, heart damage, nervous system damage, or crippling arthritis—and she does not intend to let this happen to any of her children.

Though dealing with this illness has been a tremendous hardship on the B. family, knowledge of the signs and symptoms, combined with prompt treatment, has spared them permanent physical debility and further tragedy.

4 Signs and Symptoms

Lyme disease's great range of presentations has earned it the nickname of "the Great Imitator." The importance of knowing the signs and symptoms of Lyme disease cannot be overstressed because it mimics the symptoms of about eighty other illnesses, including arthritis, Alzheimer's disease, and heart disease. When doctors speak of Lyme disease, they often refer to it as having "protean clinical manifestations," which means that the disease's "changeability" is manifested in diverse ways. Symptoms can be highly variable from one person to another, and, over time, can also vary dramatically in one person. Most commonly, Lyme disease is mistaken for the flu.

Although there is a classic pattern of illness in Lyme disease, it is not seen in nearly half of all patients. Absence of a pattern can make spotting the disease extraordinarily difficult and living with it frustrating and painful.

THE THREE STAGES OF LYME DISEASE

Typically, Lyme disease has three stages: rash and flu-like illness, heart and nervous system problems, and arthritis.

The first stage is heralded by the telltale rash, the most common characteristic of Lyme disease. (A persistent sore throat and dry cough may appear several days before the rash.) In 60 percent of the cases, the rash is accompanied by fever, fatigue, and muscle aches and/or headache. The reddened area may be warm, itchy, tender, and/or "doughy."

The rash appears at the bite location from two days to a few weeks after the bite. It usually starts as a small red spot that expands as the spirochetes spread beyond the bite area. Most commonly, the rash develops into a reddish circle or oval about 2 to 3 inches (5 to 7.6 cm) in diameter. It goes unnoticed by about a third of all patients because it fades—with or without treatment—after a few weeks. Much larger rashes—anywhere from 6 to 20 inches (15 to 51 cm) in diameter—may also occur, especially on the back. Despite their size, larger rashes may also go unnoticed because they are often faint.

The most common skin reaction and the clearest indicator of Lyme disease is the "bull's-eye" rash. This rash consists of red rings resembling a target. Another rash often seen is that of a red circle with a clear center. The rashes change in shape and size depending on

The ECM rash can be very faint and barely noticeable or, as seen here, large, red, and in a bull's-eye pattern.

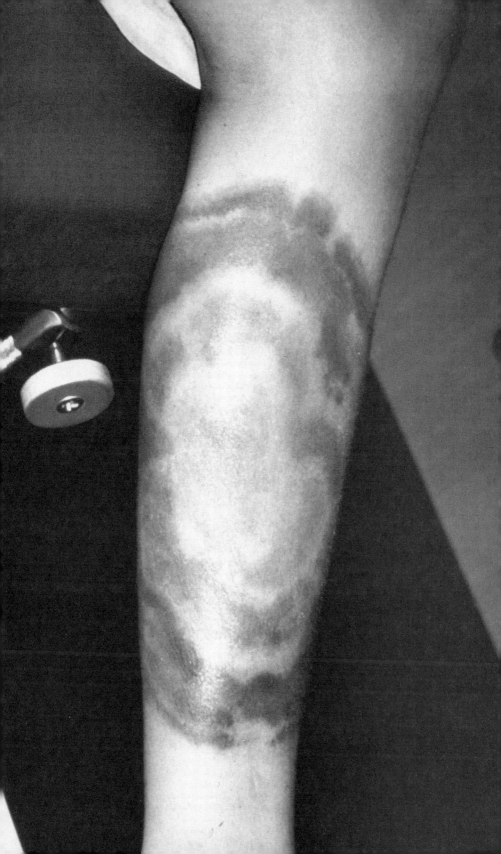

their location on the body. The most common places that these rashes appear are the thigh, groin, and armpits, and it is not uncommon for rashes to develop in more than one place.

In three to four weeks, the lesions are replaced by small red blotches that persist for several more weeks. The feelings of illness and fatigue are constant, but other symptoms are not always present. Less common effects are meningitislike symptoms, complex neuropsychiatric disorders, migrating muscle and skeletal pain, and hepatitis.

The early flulike symptoms, such as headache, chills, fever, fatigue, and muscle aches, can often trick victims into ignoring the real problem and not seeking treatment or can trick doctors into making a wrong diagnosis. Careful attention should be paid to such symptoms because tick bites don't always produce a rash, and the flulike symptoms may be the only warning signs to alert you to see a doctor—especially if they occur in summer and you live in an area that is endemic for Lyme disease.

If treatment is not obtained during the first stage, the disease quickly degenerates into the second stage. Almost one-fifth of all patients who go untreated suffer acute nervous system and heart problems. Sometimes the disease mimics Bell's palsy by causing paralysis of one or both sides of the face. In the majority of patients the usual second-stage symptoms are rapid or abnormal heartbeat, light-headedness, difficulty breathing, severe headache, encephalitis, and meningitis.

The most common heart problem associated with Lyme disease is heart block, caused by irregularity in the electrical impulses that regulate the heart. While fear of a heart attack may force the patient to the hospital, it is not likely that Lyme disease will be diagnosed unless the doctor suspects it and tests for it. These heart problems usually disappear in a week or two, but are sometimes prolonged, requiring the use of a temporary pacemaker to help regulate the patient's heartbeat. The nervous system problems usually subside in anywhere from a few days to a few months.

Stage three begins months or even years later and is most often characterized by disabling arthritis. In the third stage, about 50 percent of all untreated patients develop arthritis in the knees. Episodes are usually cyclical; they last for several weeks or months, then diminish, and then recur.

Late-stage Lyme disease also involves brain and nervous system complications that may not appear until months or years after the patient is first bitten. Patient complaints are severe and depressing fatigue, intermittent burning or numbness in the arms and legs, and problems with short-term memory. The disease has also been known to attack the liver, eyes, kidneys, spleen, and lungs. Chronic arthritis has caused destruction of bone and cartilage in 15 percent of Lyme disease–related arthritis cases. In 23 percent of all cases, patients develop severe neurological complications, and many experts believe the actual percentage is much higher. Some experts fear that some people with relatively mild cases of Lyme disease may yet experience serious neurological problems long after the initial infection. Such cases fuel the "time bomb" theory—that bacteria can remain latent for years in brain tissue, escaping destruction by antibiotic therapy.

The dreaded complications are most likely to occur in those whose illness has been misdiagnosed and therefore mistreated, or not diagnosed and treated promptly enough to avert complications. Even those who have been treated for Lyme disease may be stricken by these disorders. They may appear early and be properly ascribed to Lyme disease, or they may not appear for years, and by then may be misdiagnosed and improperly treated, creating more problems and aggravating the conditions. In general, most complications of Lyme disease seem to cluster in four areas where spirochetes can hide and lie dormant, thereby avoiding antibiotic therapy: the joints, the brain, the nervous system, and the heart.

DETECTION AND DIAGNOSIS

Lyme disease triggers a complex immune response in the body. Sometimes in an attempt to combat the infection, the immune system damages healthy tissue. Because patients exposed to an infection have antibodies in their blood serum that react to an agent, an antibody test can be a good indicator of infection.

B. burgdorferi is a typical spirochete: it is a unicellular, loosely coiled, left-handed helix (that is, it coils in a counterclockwise direction). Its length varies, but it usually averages 30 micrometers (thousandths of a millimeter; 1 millimeter equals .0394 inches) with seven turns of the coil. Like most spirochetes, it is small and difficult to detect; the diameter of the cell ranges from .18 to .25 micrometers, allowing it to pass through many filters designed to retain bacteria.

Detection of the spirochete in mammalian tissue is difficult. Not only is the spirochete extremely small, but normally it is present in very low numbers. Two types of test are currently used: the IFA (immunofluorescence assay) and the ELISA (enzyme-linked immunosorbent assay). Both tests are very limited.

IFAs, the preferred method of detection, mix killed *B. burgdorferi* spirochetes with a patient's blood

*An electron micrograph
of a spirochete*

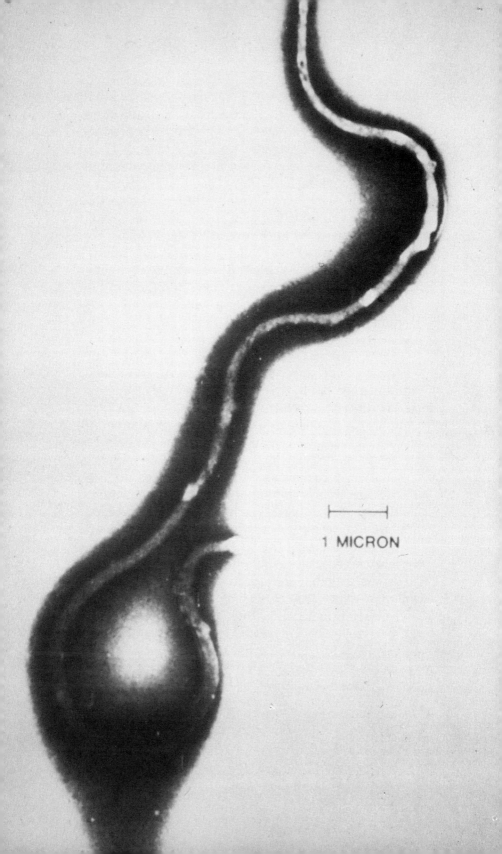

1 MICRON

sample on a microscope slide. If there are antibodies in the blood, they will attach themselves to the dead spirochetes. In order to see them clearly, a fluorescent chemical, called a reagent, is added that binds to the antibodies. These glow when illuminated with ultraviolet light, making it possible to detect the presence of even a few spirochetes. (Such studies indicate that *Borrelia* travels widely once it enters the bloodstream; it has been detected in the eyes, kidneys, spleen, liver, testes, and brain of nonhuman mammalian hosts.)

The ELISA test identifies *Borrelia* organisms using a reagent that changes color, and the depth of the color change is assessed by a machine. This test requires a very expensive and sophisticated laboratory facility.

Fortunately, Lyme disease can be treated successfully at any stage with broad-spectrum antibiotics administered orally, including penicillin, tetracycline, and erythromycin. Current studies suggest that cephalosporin antibiotics are also effective. Treatment during the first stage can greatly reduce the likelihood of developing neurological, cardiac, or arthritic complications. Even if Lyme disease is left untreated until the third stage, it can still be eradicated in most patients by antibiotic therapy, although hospitalization and intravenous administration may be necessary at this stage.

(Physicians who treat patients with Lyme disease have observed an unusual phenomenon. Immediately following antibiotic therapy there is a temporary worsening of symptoms. This phenomenon, known as the Jarisch–Herxheimer reaction, was first seen in syphilis patients who were treated with mercury ointments in the sixteenth century. Syphilis is also caused by a spirochete, *Trepnema palladum,* and it shares many of the symptoms of Lyme disease, including rashes, joint pain, and neurological complications.)

For the most part, the early symptoms of Lyme

disease are relatively mild and are controllable with antibiotics. But for those who go too long without treatment, or who don't respond to antibiotics, a recurrence of limb numbness, facial palsy, seizures, and excruciating headaches can occur.

Although Lyme disease is not now regarded as fatal, it is responsible for at least two deaths—one heart-related and the other involving severe pneumonia. One patient, a man in his thirties, nearly died from neurological complications.

5 Treatment and Precautions

Although Lyme disease is hard to detect and diagnose, patients respond well to antibiotic therapy once the disease is discovered. Public education about early detection and treatment is vital.

Because the Lyme-disease spirochete is so rapidly distributed to all parts of the body once it enters the bloodstream, the antibiotic chosen must be able to penetrate all tissues in adequate concentrations in order to effectively destroy the bacteria. Since the spirochete has a very long generation time and may have periods of dormancy, treatment should be given until all the active symptoms, especially in late-stage infections, are eradicated. There is no universally effective antibiotic for the treatment of Lyme disease; standardized regimens do not exist. Treatment must be tailored to suit the individual patient.

Of the three types of antibiotics effective against Lyme disease, the tetracyclines are fairly effective at the beginning stages of Lyme disease but are ineffective in battling the bacteria present in the later stages of the disease. Penicillins are active bacteria killers and thus have a better track record for treating advanced cases of Lyme disease. Erythromycin does not fight this spirochete very well and is only used after all else has failed.

If you find and remove an embedded deer tick, but have none of the previously mentioned signs or symptoms, you are not necessarily out of danger. Many victims did not develop either the characteristic rash or any of the other symptoms for several months, then developed the more prominent physical symptoms of Lyme disease—at which point the disease was advanced and very difficult to treat. So although some experts recommend only careful observation, other authorities recommend that asymptomatic patients be given preventive treatment, just as if all of the symptoms of Lyme disease were actually present.

Your doctor's decision to treat or not would most likely be based on the type of tick, whether it came from an area endemic for Lyme disease, and how long the tick was attached. Nymphs need to be embedded for at least one day, and more likely three days, in order to transmit Lyme disease, but adult ticks can transmit the disease in as little as four hours. The costs and risks of treatment must also be weighed against the risks of not treating a symptom that *may* evolve into late Lyme disease.

Regardless of which regimen is followed, treatment will fail if the patient does not follow doctor's orders, uses alcohol on a regular basis, or does not obtain sufficient rest. (A patient should take a break when, or ideally before, the inevitable mid-afternoon fatigue sets in.)

All patients should keep a carefully detailed daily diary of their symptoms to help judge the effects of

treatment. There is currently no test that will indicate when all the disease has been eradicated, so further testing assumes a major role in Lyme disease care.

If you feel any of the following symptoms as part of a current illness, you should consider the possibility of having contracted Lyme disease.

1. Tick bite (deer tick or dog tick)
2. Body rashes
3. Rash at the bite site
4. Unexplained fevers, chills, sweating
5. Unexplained weight change (loss or gain)
6. Fatigue
7. Unexplained hair loss
8. Swollen glands
9. Sore throat
10. Testicular pain or pelvic pain
11. Unexplained menstrual irregularity
12. Irritable bladder or bladder dysfunction
13. Upset stomach
14. Change in bowel function (constipation, diarrhea)
15. Chest pain or rib soreness
16. Shortness of breath or coughing
17. Swelling of the joints
18. Muscle pain or cramps
19. Twitching of the face or other muscles
20. Headache
21. Neck creaks and stiffness

This young woman with Lyme disease must administer her own medication several times a day for periods of up to three weeks at a time.

22. Stiffness of the joints or back
23. Tingling, numbness, burning, or stabbing sensations
24. Facial paralysis (Bell's palsy)
25. Double or blurry vision, pain in the eyes, increased floaters
26. Ear pain and buzzing or ringing
27. Dizziness, poor balance, increased motion sickness
28. Lightheadedness, wooziness, difficulty walking
29. Nervous tics or tremors, or uncontrolled shaking
30. Confusion, difficulty in concentrating or reading
31. Decreased short-term memory
32. Disorientation: getting lost, going to the wrong place
33. Speech difficulties
34. Irritability, depression, or mood swings
35. Disturbed sleep or early awakening

While each of these symptoms, alone or even with one or two others, does not necessarily mean Lyme disease, it is a particularly good idea to rule out other causes if you live in any of the geographical areas that are infested with Lyme disease or in an area where you can see deer often. Unless a patient actually remembers being bitten by a tick or developing the characteristic rash, it is nearly impossible to diagnose early-stage Lyme disease. Blood tests are not helpful until antibodies form, some four to eight weeks after exposure. Even then, tests are not standardized and are sometimes inconclusive. False negatives and lab errors do occur. On the other hand, a positive test does not necessarily mean that the patient has the disease; it simply indicates the presence of antibodies to the Lyme disease bacterium.

If treatment is given early during stage one, most patients recover completely. If the disease progresses to its later stages, some tissue damage may be irrevers-

During this checkup, a young patient's pulse is monitored by an assistant while the doctor writes out a prescription.

ible. It is not known whether the damage is done by the spirochete itself or by the immune system's response. Even with an adequate treatment, however, symptoms can recur, although later attacks tend to be less severe. Follow-up blood tests showing declining Lyme disease blood-serum levels are considered an indication that the illness was successfully treated. Some patients, however, continue to show an elevated blood-serum level, and clinicians are unsure about the significance of those elevated levels. Although one bout of Lyme disease does not grant immunity, it is thought to make the patient more resistant to the disease. However, in the case of Lyme disease, prevention is the only real protection.

PREVENTION PRECAUTIONS

The *I. dammini* tick lives in grassy, sandy, and wooded areas. During its two-year lifespan, it survives by sucking blood from warm-blooded animals. As mentioned before, the tick contracts the disease by feeding on its favorite prey, the spirochete-infected deer and field mice. Then during its nymphal stage, which lasts from May to August, the tick will most likely attach itself to an unsuspecting person walking through tall underbrush, or even across a lawn.

It's possible to get Lyme disease at any time of the year, but the incidence, at least in the northern part of the United States, is greatest in the summer. You should take precautions all year round, especially after heavy rains followed by warm weather. It is also possible to get Lyme disease anywhere, which eliminates the best way you may have thought of to avoid it: staying away from the known infested areas. The best and only way to avoid infection is to avoid ticks. But recent studies have shown that this may not be as easy as it seems because infected ticks may lurk right out-

*Here, the deer tick is barely
visible on a field mouse, one of the
creature's favorite host animals.*

side your doorstep. The Centers for Disease Control recommends the following precautions:

Clothing

- Always wear shoes and socks and never wear open sandals during the first weeks of tick and flea season.
- Wear long pants, and cinch them at the ankles or tuck them into boots or socks in particularly dangerous areas.
- Wear light-colored clothing so that ticks will be easier to see.
- Use a repellent. Repellents containing DEET (diethyltoluamide) or Permanone are very effective. Some repellents should be applied only to clothing, not to your skin, so be sure to read directions carefully.

Close to Home

- Lawns should be treated with an insecticide specific to ticks and fleas. (It takes a week or two for the insecticide to take effect, so full protective clothing should be worn during that time. You may return to wearing warm-weather attire after the waiting period.)
- Wear gloves when gardening.

People who spend much time outdoors, such as this appropriately dressed hiker, are most at risk for contracting Lyme disease.

WARNING

AVOID TICKS!

ACTUAL SIZE

WHY?

Ticks carry microorganisms that cause serious and sometimes fatal disease in humans.

WHERE?

Ticks are most common in undeveloped brushy, lightly wooded or tall-grass areas. They climb vegetation 6 to 24 inches high along animal trails and paths and wait for wild animals, dogs, or people to brush against them.

HOW?

Avoid brushing against plants along trails, paths or little-used roadways. Look for and remove ticks from your clothing during the day and your body before bedtime. Remove crawling ticks by hand (they will not bite) and attached ticks with tweezers. Apply antiseptic.

Warning signs are often posted in areas endemic to Lyme disease.

Pets

- Always check pets for ticks.
- When tick and flea season arrives, use insecticides both inside and outside the house. Your pets can bring ticks into your home and the insects can easily move from the animal to you.
- Bathe pets with flea and tick shampoo regularly, and use flea and tick powders, sprays, and collars.

Hiking and Camping

- Stay in the middle of trails and paths, away from tick-bearing bushes and grass.
- When camping, sweep the ground before setting up, and be generous with insecticides and repellents.

Body Checks

- Check yourself and your pets carefully for ticks after any outdoor activity.
- Pay particular attention to your feet, ankles, and lower legs, carefully checking the skin creases around the joints where ticks like to feed.
- Remember, a tick bite may not draw your attention, and in the spring ticks are as small as the dot on an *i*. Even in the summer and fall, when they are larger, you still have to look hard to spot one: a nymph may look like a blood blister with legs, and is the size of a sesame seed.

Remember that you can contract Lyme disease no matter where you live and regardless of whether or not you have pets. Knowledge is the best protection. Be informed and take precautions.

HOW TO REMOVE A TICK

Once a tick has bitten, you must act immediately, but with proper care. Any good procedure needs to work fast in order to get the tick off before it has time to inject spirochetes into your body. The mouthparts that penetrate the skin don't harbor spirochetes. Spirochetes are injected through the mouth from the insect's stomach. The sooner you remove the tick the better, even though there might be a grace period.

Suffocating ticks with nail polish or Vaseline is not a good idea. Never use gasoline or kerosene or hot matches or lit cigarettes. They can cause injury or infection and will force the tick to dig deeper into the skin and provoke it to inject spirochetes.

To safely avoid problems, use tweezers or small forceps, which you can buy in a surgical supply store or pharmacy. Forceps are ideal. Grasp the tick on the skin, close to its mouth (which is sticking into the skin) and pull, without jerking, steadily upward. It's okay if you rip out a little skin while removing the tick.

Once the tick is removed, clean and disinfect the bite area. Put the tick in alcohol and see your doctor immediately. Give your doctor the tick for examination and watch carefully for any symptoms. Remember, early treatment can save you from a great deal of misery.

6 Current Research

Lyme disease is not as mysterious as it was when first discovered, but it still is a "mystery disease" because it is constantly perplexing physicians. Research is attempting to solve some of these mysteries, such as why patients experience so many symptoms despite the presence of only a small number of spirochetes.

Two theories are being studied. The first theory holds that groups of immune factors consisting of antigens from the spirochete, antibodies, and a nonspecific complete group of biochemical materials from the patient accumulate in the patient's joints. This accumulation causes the release of enzymes that attack the group. According to this theory, it is these enzymes that cause many of the symptoms. The second theory proposes that the enzymes are amplified by an immune-system mediator called interleukin-1 (*IL*-1).

Testing procedures are also part of the research effort. A new test now under development that seeks out spirochete antigens in blood and urine would allow the disease to be diagnosed even before antibodies are

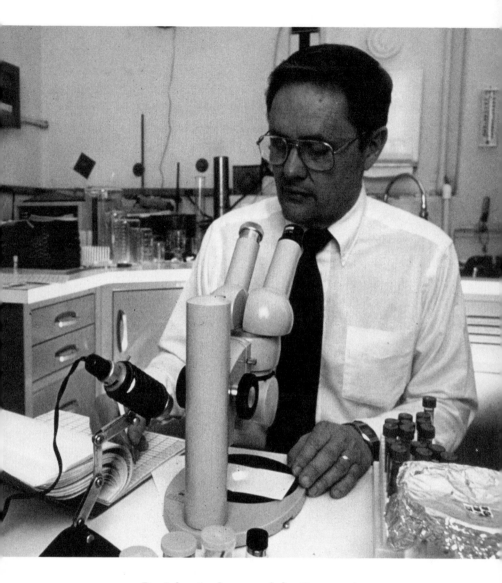

Dr. John Anderson of the Connecticut Agricultural Experiment Station records data at his lab in New Haven, Connecticut, which is a national clearinghouse for the analysis of tick and blood samples.

formed. Physicians could then begin treatment more quickly.

Also on the horizon is a test using DNA probes, such as those used to determine paternity. This test uses genetic material to detect specific organisms, such as *Borrelia burgdorferi*. If probes specific for the DNA of the Lyme bug can be found, it would be a simple but highly effective blood test.

And recently, some breakthroughs have been made in the development of a vaccine.

In the area of prevention, a product called Damminix holds promise. It is a small cardboard cylinder containing cotton treated with the pesticide permethrin. When the cylinder is laid on the ground, mice use the cotton to build nests. The pesticide is harmless to mice, but it kills the deer ticks that feed on the mice. The cost is high: over $350 a year to treat one acre (0.4 ha) of land—which makes its use impractical for individuals who may be only slightly concerned about the possible presence of the infected deer tick. Communities that are located in hot spots for Lyme disease may consider Damminix treatment a worthwhile use of municipal or county funds.

7 Other Pest-Borne Diseases

People have been subject to plagues spread by insects since the dawn of time. Because disease caused by insect-borne bacteria and spirochetes is so common, many people don't give it a second thought. They tend to think that the greatest threat to humanity is war, which has done so much to change and shape human history, but this is not so. Insect-borne diseases have killed more people than all the known wars combined.

Of these insect-borne diseases, those transmitted by fleas and ticks are more virulent than those borne by other insects. Ticks and fleas have preyed upon mammals since prehistoric times. Because of their extremely small size and their inconspicuous parasitic attacks, fleas and ticks were never really associated with the diseases they carried until the seventeenth and eighteenth centuries. Some weren't even recognized until as late as the nineteenth and twentieth centuries. Ancient man used to blame the outbreaks of flea- and tick-transmitted diseases on supernatural occurrences, witchcraft, or the wrath of the gods. Some ancient cultures even performed human sacrifices in an effort to end epidemics.

Some references in the Bible imply that bubonic plague, a virulent disease carried by rats and the fleas that live on them, may have existed as early as the sixth century, B.C., but no other proof exists. The first identification of bubonic plague was made in Egypt about the third century, B.C. There are no records of a recurrence until A.D. 542. The epidemic that occurred then was one of the earliest recorded, and is said to have changed the course of human history. It was as devastating as the more famous Black Death plague of the fourteenth century, causing a reduction in population from which it would take centuries to recover.

The Roman Empire had fallen, and its territory was split up into the Eastern and Western Empires. Justinian, the emperor of the Eastern, or Byzantine, Empire, had amassed troops to try to reunify the Roman Empire. But, in the empire's capital city of Constantinople alone, ten thousand people died every day for four months from this plague. Justinian's troops were wiped out—not by war but by disease. This scourge was the major cause of the collapse of the Eastern Roman Empire, and allowed the Muslims to take over almost a century later in A.D. 634.

The bubonic plague also spread to China in A.D. 610. Although much of the rat population was decimated by the disease it carried, a number of the infected rats survived the long sea journey from the Mediterranean, or the shorter but more dangerous journey overland, to bring the plague thousands of miles to China. In 762 a series of epidemics broke out, killing more than half the population in Shantung Province. Another outbreak occurred with equal devastation in 806, this time in Chekiang Province, again carrying off half the population. In all, it is estimated that 2.4 million households were destroyed. These outbreaks are viewed by historians as a possible cause of the collapse of central authority in China, destroying a once powerful culture and making it vulnerable to later invasion by nomadic steppe tribes.

Meanwhile, in Europe outbreaks of the plague were diminishing, and by 767 it had virtually disappeared. In the fourteenth century, however, the epidemic known as the Black Death suddenly erupted, wiping out entire hamlets and villages at a time. It was especially virulent in the cities, with their high rat population. Though this tragedy first struck in the 1340s, it persisted for many years in both Europe and the Mideast.

From 1346 to 1350, one-third of Europe's population was wiped out by the Black Death. After 1350, the plague recurred continuously despite strict quarantines. The last major outbreaks occurred in 1720 and 1721 around the Marseilles area in France.

When the plague broke out again in China between 1894 and 1921, careful medical study and strict preventive measures kept it from becoming a worldwide epidemic that could have killed millions. Since then antibiotics have helped contain outbreaks, but to this day occasional strains persist in various remote areas of the world.

The second parasite-borne disease that has had a great effect on history is typhus, which is transmitted to humans by fleas, ticks, and lice. Typhus was an

This engraving shows the protective clothing worn by doctors who treated the plague during the seventeenth century.

infection that assumed spectacular form during the age of oceanic exploration from the years 1450 to 1550, and then spread to Europe as a byproduct of war. Typhus was first identified in Europe in 1490, when it was brought to Spain by soldiers fighting in Cyprus. Then it was spread to Italy by Spanish soldiers who were waging war against the French for control of Italy. In 1526, an outbreak of typhus forced French troops to end their seige of Naples and withdraw. Typhus is important in military history because of its disruptive effect on army life—and the duration of war itself. Though it seems to occur most often during wartime, its major victims, however, appear to be the poor. Typhus is a disease associated with poverty and the resulting overcrowding, unsanitary living conditions, and inadequate medical care.

In 1813 and 1814, one-tenth of the entire German population contracted typhus and one percent died during a single epidemic. In the 1840s, an outbreak of typhus, accompanied by widespread famine, resulted in millions of deaths as well as major emigrations of Irish, Belgians, and Germans to the shores of the United States and Latin America. Typhus then emerged in North America and was brought into the western United States along with the waves of settlers looking for new farmland.

Typhus was especially virulent during the Industrial Revolution from 1750 to 1850, killing more soldiers than the lengthy Napoleonic Wars that were being waged at that same time. Living conditions in the newly industrialized towns and cities of the day were notoriously filthy, with inadequate waste removal and sewage disposal. The advent of the Napoleonic Wars created new stresses that exposed these societies to epidemics. Urban slums were constantly being decimated by typhus, as were jails, poorhouses, and even sick wards for the poor. These conditions lasted until World War I, when 2 to 3 million people died of typhus.

While typhus was raging through the slums of Europe, a discovery was made between 1909 and 1912 that allowed the chiefs of states of Europe to continue their military plans uninterrupted. Simple though it may seem, the major breakthrough of the time was cleanliness. Delousing stations were instituted, soldiers were required to bathe and shampoo regularly, and clean clothing for the troops was provided on a regular basis. These measures considerably cut down the spread of the disease, and thousands of soldiers—who would have been the natural victims of typhus—lost their lives in battle instead. Typhus was also a major contributor to the death and destruction that accompanied the Russian Revolution in 1917.

Since the discovery of antibiotics, such devastating diseases as plague and typhus have been brought under control and no longer threaten populations as they once did. But with more and more population centers encroaching on formerly rural areas, an increasing number of people—especially people who wouldn't normally think of themselves as being at risk because of their urban and suburban life-styles—are being exposed to the dangers of pest-borne diseases.

These diseases are all caused by bacteria of the genus *Rickettsia*. The route of infection for these diseases is most frequently through the skin, either being injected through the mouths of ticks or by contamination through infected louse or flea excrement onto broken skin or wounds. Another route of infection is through the lungs or eyes by means of airborne bacteria from dried, powdery flea and louse feces. All rickettsiae are highly infectious through the respiratory tract.

Thus ticks, fleas, and other parasitic creatures continue to beset humans as carriers of such diseases as Rocky Mountain spotted fever, babesiosis, relapsing fever, tick paralysis, Q fever, and the most predominant problem—Lyme disease.

RELAPSING FEVER

Relapsing fever is a systemic infection caused by spirochetes of the *Borrelia* family that are transmitted from one person to another by lice or ticks of the genus *Ornithodoros*. Relapsing fever has been known by many names throughout history, among them "yellow plague," "yellow famine fever," "vagabond fever," "bilious typhoid" and "recurring fever."

The disease is characterized by an abrupt, severe infection that lasts several days, and may recur one or more times. Each relapse is less severe than the preceding one, and of shorter duration. The infection mostly affects the spleen, liver, brain, and heart, and may seriously impair the blood's ability to coagulate.

Louse-borne relapsing fever is one of the classic epidemic diseases that has been terrorizing humans through the ages. In earlier times it was the scourge of Europe. After World War I, because of the widespread poverty, depopulation, and depression caused by years of strife, relapsing fever was responsible for the deaths of 5 million people in Europe, as well as hundreds of thousands more in Africa. During World War II, there were a million cases in North Africa, where much of the fighting took place. There were several minor outbreaks of the disease in the United States during the Great Depression of the 1930s, when hunger and poverty were widespread. Immediately following the end of World War II, from 1945 to 1947, there were a million cases of relapsing fever in Egypt alone. Between 1930 and 1947, eight percent of the people who contracted the disease died of it.

It is common to see outbreaks of both typhus and relapsing fever in poverty-stricken areas, including a surprising number of Western cities. Flea and lice infestations thrive in crowded slums, making the diseases they carry a possibility in those situations where cleanliness is not always an option.

Louse-borne relapsing fever is caused by *B. recurrentis*. Lice become infected when they feed on carrier rodents, and become infectious within five to eight days. The lice remain infected for their remaining few short weeks of life. The infection is transmitted to a human when a louse is crushed against him or her and the spirochete penetrates the skin. Great care should be taken so that lice are not crushed when being removed.

During the Great Depression, and the late 1940s and early 1950s after World War II, great care and caution were taken to screen out possible infestations of lice at schools. The children generally were not told about the typhus and relapsing fever that could be caused by passing lice from one child to another. Parents were warned to check their children's scalps frequently for lice or "nits," which are louse eggs.

There are still many medicinal shampoos and treatments on pharmacy shelves from this era, and caution should still be exercised against possible infestations. If lice or nits are found, follow the instructions of any of the special delousing treatments on the market. First, apply the product, then comb through the hair very carefully with a fine-toothed comb to remove nits, which attach themselves to the base of the hair shaft close to the scalp. Do not share combs or head wear with anyone until the scalp is again louse-free.

As mentioned, this is a serious health problem, complicated by the deep emotional trauma that is associated with lice infestations. For school officials or public health officials, the ultimate nightmare is a widespread head-lice infestation. Successful control requires cooperation among school administrators, teachers, and parents. All three groups should be educated as to the nature of the problem, diagnosis, treatment, and prevention.

SIGNS AND SYMPTOMS. Louse-borne relapsing fever incubates within two to fifteen days. Early symptoms include chills and high fever. The fever and chills continue for two or three days and are accompanied by a profound sense of weakness and tiredness, severe headaches, dizziness, and nightmares. Generalized muscle aches and pains and lower back pain are also common.

Within three days the patient becomes apathetic, has a glazed expression, a hot forehead, cold hands, and suffers from dullness or confusion. Shivering and breathlessness also occur. A rash, jaundice, and tenderness in the area over the liver occur. The rash appears most commonly on the shoulders, the sides of the torso, and the inner arms and thighs. Signs and symptoms vary from one case to another. All patients suffer from a fever and rapid heartbeat. Blood pressure is often low, and respiration rapid and difficult. Deafness and blindness occasionally develop. Delirium and coma may follow. Miscarriage is common among pregnant women who have contracted the disease. Complications from secondary infections may include pneumonia, heart infections, and diarrhea. Typhus, malaria, typhoid, and dysentery may also result.

Throughout the illness, fever remains high. After three to thirteen days, the temperature progressively drops. Complications may then develop that can be fatal. If the patient recovers, he or she may be exhausted for days.

If the illness goes untreated, the victim will "relapse" after five to seven days, followed by another attack which rarely lasts more than four days. Each reoccurrence is less severe than the previous one, and no rash is evident. Additional relapses may follow, but rarely does a patient suffer more than four, after which he makes a gradual, but complete, recovery.

TREATMENT. Patients respond well to a course of antibiotics prescribed by a doctor, but there is a risk of a Jarisch-Herxheimer Reaction. This reaction may be a result of the sudden removal of the spirochetes from the patient's system. It is characterized by severe chills, increased metabolic rate, shock, and a high risk of heart failure. The mortality rate for relapsing fever is 4 to 40 percent, depending on if and when treatment occurs. Early treatment reduces the likelihood of complications and death.

PREVENTION. During an outbreak, it is necessary to initiate delousing measures as soon as possible and observe strict cleanliness and hygiene. Starting in the home, especially during warm weather, you can protect from infection by regularly using insecticides on surfaces and on pets, as well as observing stringent cleanliness in warm damp areas such as the bathroom, laundry, and kitchen areas. However, the most common risk to children is found in the school environment. Regular checking for lice, and appropriate treatment and removal should any be found, can help prevent the development of more serious problems.

TICK-BORNE RELAPSING FEVER

This illness is also known as "tick fever," as distinguished from louse-borne relapsing fever. It is not the same disease, although the symptoms are similar.

73

While louse-borne relapsing fever is common among poor and crowded populations, tick-borne relapsing fever is contracted through direct contact with ticks and their normal hosts.

In the United States, the carrier of this fever, *Ornithodoros hermsi*, is found in the forests of the Western mountains and Colorado. The organisms are associated with hibernating rodents who sleep in or near cabins and houses. *O. parker* is another vector. It is found among burrowing rodents who live in the deserts and semiarid plains, and tends to infect hunters and vacationers. A third vector is *O. turicata*, which largely inhabits caves in Texas and nearby states. When goats and sheep wander into these caves, the tick seems to always find them.

In Mediterranean countries, another culprit is *O. erraticus*. This tick is not as choosy as its American counterparts. It lives in a variety of animal burrows, and attacks both settled and nomadic peoples. Another tick is *O. tholozani*, which, like its Texan cousin, prefers to live in caves and burrows. The ticks infest a wide variety of fowl, sheep, camels, and other hosts, and so the fever is easily passed along travel routes and spread from one population group to another.

Of the many ticks which harbor and spread tick-borne relapsing fever, *O. moubata* has the closest contact with humans. It is found in central, eastern, and southern Africa, where it inhabits only the savannah regions. It lives in the cracks and crevices of the earthen floors of people's houses, and at night crawls out of its dark hiding place to feed on the inhabitants.

SIGNS AND SYMPTOMS. The incubation period for tick fever is four to eighteen days, and the disease runs the same course as the louse-borne infection, with the additional risk of neurological complications. These include eye pain, dimness of vision, coma, convulsions, nerve lesions, nightmares, hallucinations, severe anxiety, and depression. These complications are common in late relapses.

The Mediterranean, Mideastern, and American strains of the disease are less severe than the African strain. Fever is the primary symptom and neurological problems disappear quickly.

Tick-borne relapsing fever is not usually as severe as louse-borne relapsing fever. If it is not properly treated, however, it will be prolonged and cause severe debilitation. Death is then a greater risk, occurring in 5 to 27 percent of all cases.

TREATMENT. This disease responds very well to tetracycline but not to penicillin.

PREVENTION. Liberal use of insecticides keeps ticks under control. Outside the home, the generous use of repellents, combined with all the Lyme disease precautions, such as proper clothing and body checks, provides a high degree of protection. In the Rocky Mountains, homes and cabins should be made rodent proof. Safeguards should also be taken to control the rodent population within twenty yards of the building. Bedding should be treated every spring. There is no vaccine for tick-borne relapsing fever.

TICK PARALYSIS

A severe problem that occasionally develops from tick bites is a progressive paralysis that ascends through the body, beginning with the extremities. It occurs in humans and both wild and domestic animals. The paralysis is caused by a toxin released by attached female hard ticks while they feed. It is believed that the toxin is injected into the body after the tick is attached and has been feeding for one or more days. Several species have been associated with the disease, but in the United States, the culprits are the Rocky Mountain wood tick and the American dog tick.

The disease begins with restlessness, irritability, and numbness or tingling in the hands and/or legs, lips, throat, and face. Soon the victim has difficulty walking. This is soon followed by an inability to stand. Within one or two days, paralysis of the limbs and trunk sets in, which leads to slurred speech, difficulty in swallowing, and impaired vision. The diagnosis of tick paralysis is tricky because often the tick bite is painless and goes unnoticed by the patient. As a further difficulty in making the diagnosis, the tick is usually hidden in the patient's hair and goes unnoticed by the physician. Also, blood tests show nothing significant, and fever rarely occurs. The symptoms of tick paralysis resemble those of polio and may be misdiagnosed, resulting in the wrong course of treatment for the disease.

Diagnosis may also be further delayed because of the rarity of the condition. It is not often seen, even though cases pop up now and then in Oregon, Washington, Oklahoma, Arkansas, Mississippi, North Carolina, Virginia, and other states. Most cases involve children and teenagers, with death occurring in 10 to 12 percent of the cases. The deaths usually result from respiratory paralysis.

Treatment consists of simply removing the tick. Recovery is usually rapid and complete within a few hours or days.

In Australia, an antitick serum for dogs is available. In other areas, the same prevention measures and precautions as for Lyme diseases should be followed, as well as the same tick-removal technique.

EPIDEMIC TYPHUS FEVER

Also known as "Classic," "Historic," and "European typhus," and as "Jail," "War," "Ship" and "Camp Fever," this disease is an acute infectious disease transmitted by lice. It begins with the sudden onslaught of long-lasting high fever of about two weeks duration, a rash, and an altered mental state. Months, or even years later, a condition called Brill-Zinsser disease sets in. It is caused by organisms which have persisted in the tissues since the initial infection, and this latter disease resembles a mild form of typhus. The bacteria involved in both the initial condition and the secondary one is *Rickettsia prowazekii.*

TRANSMISSION. Typhus is classically transmitted to humans from lice, not through bites, but by dying after burrowing underneath the skin, by being crushed, or by depositing feces in bite sites or other breaks in the skin. It can also be contracted through the respiratory tract.

Typhus can occur anywhere in the world, but occurs most frequently under conditions of poverty and overcrowding, which allows for the close contact lice need to be transferred from person to person.

SIGNS AND SYMPTOMS. Typhus has an incubation period of eight to twelve days, but it can be as short as six days and as long as fifteen. The disease may be divided into three phases: the forerunner, the early phase, and the late phase.

Initial forerunners can include weariness and headaches.

The early phase is ushered in by the quick onset of fever, severe headache, pain in the back and legs, and chills. The headache is intense, and persists day and night. Fever remains high with only slight fluctuations until death or recovery. The skin is usually hot and dry, and the face is flushed. Patients frequently have a painful reaction to light. Deafness, ear pain, and vertigo also occur. Weakness and exhaustion are mild at first, but worsen after two or three days. A dry cough is very common.

In the late phase, after four to seven days, a rash appears. It first appears on the trunk and folds of the arms and spreads to the legs and the rest of the arms. The lesions are pinkish red and whiten when pressure is applied. The rash may last from two days to two weeks, depending on the severity of the illness. Pulse rates range from slow to rapid, and blood pressure is unusually low. The mental state progresses from dullness to stupor, and sometimes, to coma.

If the patient recovers, the temperature begins to decline after fourteen to eighteen days; otherwise, death occurs between the ninth and the eighteenth day.

Vascular decay—blood vessels that collapse and die under unbroken skin—is common, along with secondary infections. Such decay results in gangrene, which is fatal in itself unless the infected part is healed or removed.

Depending on the patient's age and condition before contracting the disease, the mortality rate ranges from 10 to 60 percent. Deep coma, along with low blood pressure and rapid heartbeat, are signs of a poor prognosis.

TREATMENT. Long-acting antibiotics are very effective in most cases, leading to recovery in two to three days, regardless of when treatment is begun. If this were not a disease that affects the poor, it probably could have been eradicated by now, since treatment is so effective. Because of the expense, however, the poor seldom seek medical treatment.

PREVENTION AND CONTROL. Strict cleanliness in endemic areas and around affected or suspect populations, and the liberal use of pesticides, will reduce the possibility of contracting typhus. Though classic typhus is seldom seen in the United States, the conditions for its potential advent are being set up through the rising population of homeless individuals and families. These people have no way of controlling the cleanliness of their environments, and no way of eliminating insect pests from their immediate surroundings. Conditions like these invite an outbreak of classic typhus epidemics.

MURINE TYPHUS FEVER

Murine typhus is an acute infectious disease communicable from rodents to humans by means of the rodents' fleas. Murine typhus is not communicable between humans. It is not transmitted by bite, but by the contamination of broken skin with infectious feces or by the inhalation of dried feces from infected rodents.

Murine typhus occurs worldwide. In the United States, incidences mostly occur when fleas are in abundance during the summer. Wherever rats come into contact with humans, typhus can be contracted.

SIGNS AND SYMPTOMS. The incubation period of murine typhus is six to fourteen days. The symptoms are similar to louse-borne typhus, except that murine is a milder disease. The rash is less extensive, there are fewer complications, the fatality rate is lower, and the recovery time is shorter. In untreated cases, the mortality rate is 5 percent, but with treatment, the rate is zero percent.

PREVENTION. For people who work in areas where rats and their fleas abound, it is recommended that clothing treated with flea repellent be worn. Major rat control measures are also recommended, along with pesticides to control their fleas.

ROCKY MOUNTAIN SPOTTED FEVER

Rocky Mountain spotted fever, also called tick typhus or spotted fever, is an acute infectious disease that is sometimes fatal. It is caused by the bacteria *Rickettsia ricketsii*, transmitted by several species of ticks.

Originally observed in the Rocky Mountain states, which is how it got its name, Rocky Mountain spotted fever has been recognized in forty-six states and is actually more prevalent in the southern Atlantic states than in the western mountain states. While it can be found from Cape Cod, Massachusetts, all the way to Florida, over half the cases in the United States occur in Maryland, Virginia, North Carolina, and Georgia. The spread of Rocky Mountain spotted fever follows the same pattern as Lyme disease. Rocky Mountain spotted fever has also been recognized in Canada, Mexico, Central America, Colombia, and Brazil. It seems to be confined to the Western Hemisphere; there have been no reports from Europe or Asia of ticks infected with this particular rickettsia and spreading it to humans.

The disease is spread to humans by ticks which are introduced into the human environment by small and large mammals. Humans become infected when they accidentally come into contact with rodents and are bitten by an infected tick. Dogs can also bring infected ticks into the human environment. The culprits in Rocky Mountain spotted fever are the wood tick in the western United States, the dog tick in the eastern states, and the brown dog tick in Texas and Oklahoma.

SIGNS AND SYMPTOMS. Many patients, but not all, are aware of a tick bite. Incubation is from two to fourteen days depending on the severity of the case. Attacks can be so mild that the victims ignore the symptoms, or they can be so severe that death occurs in three to six days. Symptoms begin with severe headache, chills, fever, exhaustion, back and leg pain, nausea, vomiting, and sensitivity to light. A high fever begins in two days and lasts for about two weeks.

The characteristic rash appears about the fourth day, beginning on the wrists and ankles and then extending over all or most of the body. At first the rash is pink and turns white when pressure is applied. In two or three days the rash darkens. Central nervous system effects include restlessness, insomnia, delirium, stupor, and in severe cases, coma. Convulsions may also occur, and jaundice is not uncommon. Convalescence may take weeks to months.

PROGNOSIS. Rocky Mountain spotted fever in any form, mild or severe, should be regarded as a major medical emergency. Mortality rates range from 10 to 60 percent. Even with treatment, mortality rates remain at 5 to 10 percent. Most deaths result mainly from a delay in seeking treatment. Since death can occur within three to six days, the period when treatment can affect outcome is very short and does not leave much room for error if a mistake is made in diagnosis.

TREATMENT. Antibiotics are the preferred treatment. Antimicrobals have little effect.

PREVENTION. Prevention measures for Rocky Mountain spotted fever are the same as for Lyme disease. Tick checks should be a daily routine for people living in tick-infested areas. Children should be carefully inspected after playing outdoors, especially during the summer months. Dogs should be regularly cared for to prevent them from carrying ticks into their masters' homes. Liberal use of insecticides will help to keep ticks under control.

Q FEVER

Of all the tick-borne diseases, one stands out as unique, because it is not transmitted to humans by tick bites. This disease, Q fever, is a self-limiting rickettsial infection.

Q fever is found to be transmitted from wild animals to domestic animals such as sheep and cattle, and then, by a secondary means of infection, from the domestic animals to humans. Most infections come from exposure to infected cattle, sheep, and goats. In sheep, infection can be transmitted by sweat, saliva, milk, and feces. In cattle and goats it can be transmitted by milk. Airborne infection can also contaminate uninfected animals in herds, and the humans who come into close contact with these herds. Airborne infection can also occur through contaminated clothing, wool, hides, bedding, and soil.

Outbreaks of Q fever have been seen in medical schools where students work with sheep and cattle in laboratories, and Q fever is a recognized laboratory hazard.

Q fever is one of the many reasons why the milk we drink is pasteurized; the disease has been found in unpasteurized milk and has been transmitted to humans who drink raw milk.

SIGNS AND SYMPTOMS. The incubation period for Q fever lasts from ten to twenty-eight days. It begins with high fever, headache, muscle pain, and severe feeling of illness. In contrast to other rickettsial diseases, Q fever does not cause a rash. In up to half of all patients, dry cough develops, and the risk of pneumonia becomes high. Other complications can include severe infections of the heart and brain. Convalescence lasts several months.

Q fever is sometimes mistaken for flu, mononucleosis, typhoid, viral pneumonia, or Legionnaires' disease. However, Q fever should be suspected if the patient has been in contact with cattle, sheep, goats, or their wool or hides. Tetracycline and chloramphenicol are effective in treating Q fever. The mortality rate is low, but occasional relapses can occur. The recovery period is lengthy.

The only control measure is that of limiting exposure, which is not practical except in laboratory environments. Pasteurizing or boiling milk from cattle, sheep, and goats is recommended in areas where Q fever is known to exist endemically.

PLAGUE

There are two forms of plague. The first, bubonic plague, is transmitted to humans by the bite of plague-infested rodent fleas. The second, called pneumonic plague, is the communicable form, transmitted from human to human. This latter form is a complication of the lungs and enters the body through the respiratory tract.

Plague is caused by the bacteria *Versinia pestis*. Known as the "Black Death" in the fourteenth century, this vicious infection killed millions of human beings.

Plague is endemic in Vietnam, other parts of

Southeast Asia, India, Burma, Java, and South Central and East Africa. The disease has also erupted occasionally in Egypt, Saudi Arabia, North Africa, and South America. It is also found in the western and southwestern United States.

The World Health Organization reported that at the peak outbreak of plague in the twentieth century, only 5,000 cases were reported. Most of them were in Vietnam. In the United States, there has been a steady increase, now an average of eleven cases a year.

TRANSMISSION AND HOST RANGE. Plague naturally occurs among both domestic and wild rodents. Fleas become infected with *V. pestis* when they feed on an infected rat, and then the disease is transmitted in a rodent-to-flea-to-rodent cycle. If another rodent is not available, the fleas will find a different mammalian host, including humans. Thus humans become the accidental hosts—we are not the fleas' first choice of meals.

If the plague is introduced into small mammal or other rodent populations, such as prairie dogs or bats, it is called "Epizootic plague." These animals are more susceptible to the lethal effects of infection than the rat. Humans are at very high risk if they come into contact with epizootic plague. Transmissions from animals to humans is called "zootic plague." Human to human transmission is called "demic plague."

In the United States, all but one case has resulted from exposure to infected animals in rural or urban environments. The main culprits have been squirrels, prairie dogs, marmots, wood rats, rabbits, and hares. Humans infected by rabbits and hares usually make direct tissue contact. Cats, dogs, and coyotes can also become infected, and can in turn infect humans. Humans can also be carriers of the disease.

SIGNS AND SYMPTOMS. One major problem in diagnosis of plague is that the signs and symptoms are not often recognized outside of endemic areas.

The most common form of this disease is bubonic plague. The incubation period may vary from a few hours to twelve days, but it is usually two to five days. The onset is abrupt, with chills and high fever. The pulse is rapid and extremely low blood pressure occurs. Painful and enlarged lymph nodes in the neck, armpits, and groin areas appear after one to four days. There are usually no marks at the site of the bite, but sometimes a small lesion can be found. Patients usually experience headaches, stomach complaints, loss of appetite, vomiting, and abdominal pain, along with restlessness, delirium, confusion, and lack of coordination.

Pneumonic plague incubates in two to three days with an abrupt onset of high fever, chills, rapid heartbeat, and severe headache. After about twenty-four hours, a productive cough develops with evidence of blood. Sputum soon becomes thick and foamy. Chest X rays will show rapidly progressing pneumonia. Untreated patients die within thirty-six to forty-eight hours after the onset of the symptoms.

TREATMENT. Upon suspicion of plague of either form, prompt treatment should reduce the mortality rate to 5 percent. Antibiotics have been highly effective.

PREVENTION. Strict rodent control and use of repellents will minimize attacks by fleas and the risk of plague infection.

There is a highly effective vaccine that is used mostly to inoculate people traveling to plague-endemic countries. If you work in an occupation that brings you into contact with rodents at any time, you should be immunized.

COLORADO TICK FEVER

Colorado tick fever is an acute, viral infection that occurs throughout the Rocky Mountains and is transmitted to humans by the bite of the hard-shelled wood tick.

The disease occurs during the spring and summer, when tick exposure is most common in the mountains. Most patients report tick bites, but as with other tick-borne diseases, many people will not be aware of the tick attachment and bite. These ticks usually feed off squirrels and chipmunks, and humans are only accidentally infected. The disease is found in most Rocky Mountain states, and in the Rocky Mountain Canadian provinces. The majority of cases, however, have been reported in Colorado. Hundreds of cases are reported in the Rocky Mountain area each year, but this may represent only a fraction of the total, as many mild cases go unreported.

The virus has been found in other species of ticks and in numerous species of small mammals, suggesting that the disease has a wider geographic distribution than was formerly thought. Colorado tick fever may be much more common than Lyme disease, but since the disease is relatively mild it is often ignored by the patients. In more severe cases, it is often misdiagnosed. Sometimes patients are infected but never experience any symptoms.

SIGNS AND SYMPTOMS. Colorado tick fever begins with chills and high fever, intense pain in the back and legs, headache, pain in the back of the eyes, and sensitivity to light. The patient may also feel tired and nauseated. Outward signs are minimal. Symptoms occur three to seven days after tick exposure. A rash over the entire body has been reported in 12 percent of all cases.

In half of all cases, a two-phase "saddle-back" fever effect occurs. Symptoms lessen after two to three days, temperature returns to normal, and the patient feels well, or nearly so, for one to two years. This is followed by an abrupt return of fever, headache, and back pain in a more intense form than in the first stage. This second phase subsides after two to four days, leaving the patient weak for a week or two. Laboratory tests, taken early in the illness, usually show nothing.

Colorado tick fever should be suspected in anyone who reports tick attachment and bite in the endemic areas (Colorado and all other Rocky Mountain states and provinces) three to seven days before the onset of the fever. If the patient experiences the "saddle-back" effect, Colorado tick fever should be strongly suspected. Lab results will confirm a diagnosis of Colorado tick fever after three to twelve days, usually during the second phase, if a "saddle-back" effect occurs.

One of the problems with differentiating Colorado tick fever from Rocky Mountain spotted fever is that they are both transmitted by the same kind of tick and in the same endemic region of the country. Colorado tick fever is actually more common than Rocky Mountain spotted fever in Colorado. There are twenty cases of Colorado tick fever for every one case of Rocky Mountain spotted fever. Detecting any difference between the two diseases is impossible in the early days of the illness before the characteristic Rocky Mountain spotted fever rash appears.

TREATMENT. There is no specific treatment. One can only make the victim as comfortable as is possible, and supply adequate fluids. Aspirin can help with the back and leg pain and the headaches, but it is not really advisable in most patients. Acetominophen can be used on a doctor's advice.

Colorado tick fever is a very benign disease and the prognosis is excellent. Severe cases with nervous system complications are usually only seen in children.

PREVENTION. The same precautions as are taken for Lyme disease are applicable to the prevention of Colorado tick fever.

BABESIOSIS

This disease was first identified by a man named Victor Babes, and named after him. In 1843, it was identified as the cause of Texas cattle fever. Then in 1904, it was discovered in humans during a Rocky Mountain spotted fever epidemic in Montana. Previously, babesiosis may have been mistaken for Rocky Mountain spotted fever. Human infection has only recently been adequately documented.

Babesiosis is caused by the protozoan *Babesia*. There are over seventy species of *Babesia*, each being host-specific. Ticks are responsible for its transmission, with *Babesia microti* being the most prevalent cause of current epidemics. This is a *Babesia* specific to rodents.

The tick responsible for the spread of rodent *Babesia* to humans is *Ixodes dammini*, the same culprit that carries Lyme disease. This is a new species of tick with feeding habits that set the pattern for human infection. Most ticks require three hosts during development, but *I. dammini* uses rodents for feeding at the larval stage, then jumps to larger mammals, such as deer or humans, for subsequent feedings.

As a newly described tick, *Ixodes dammini* has become abundant in the past few decades, and has replaced the rodent tick, *Ixodes muris*, as the dominant tick. Since *I. dammini* is widely distributed geographically, it is possible that babesiosis is as widespread as Lyme disease, although its incidence is low. It is the change in tick ecology that is possibly contributing to infection in humans. It is also possible that Lyme disease patients may become infected with babesiosis and suffer this disease as a secondary infection.

SIGNS AND SYMPTOMS. Babesiosis begins one to six weeks after a tick bite, although not many patients remember being bitten. The tick nymph usually goes unnoticed because of its small size, even though it remains attached for two to four days.

The disease begins with fatigue, chills, generalized weakness, a feeling of illness, and a loss of appetite. This is followed within a few days by an extremely high fever. This fever is accompanied by drenching sweats, chills, general pain, and joint pain. Nausea and vomiting may also occur. Several patients have displayed symptoms of depression and emotional distress. The illness may be sudden in onset, or may take up to a month before a diagnosis can be made. A rash has never been seen in any case. Though the disease is considered mild and requires no treatment, there have been fatal cases. These victims usually suffer prostration, dehydration, and kidney dysfunction. Anemia is also a complication, which shows up in the late stages of the illness.

Babesiosis should be suspected in anyone exhibiting fever from a *Babesia* endemic area. These areas are exactly the same as Lyme disease endemic areas, since *I. dammini* ticks are the culprits in both cases. Diagnosis can be confirmed through lab tests. The Centers for Disease Control has developed a blood test using *B. microti* antigens, which is very effective in making a diagnosis.

TREATMENT. As mentioned, this is a very mild disease, but in severe cases a drug called pentamidine is available from the Centers for Disease Control.

PREVENTION. Liberal use of repellents when visiting tick-infested areas and liberal use of insecticides around the home if you live in tick-disease endemic areas is helpful in limiting the transmission of the disease. Following the same precautions as is advised for Lyme disease will also help to limit the risk of infection. People who have had spleen or liver problems should take special care to avoid circumstances that might bring them into contact with infected ticks.

VIRAL ENCEPHALITIS

Encephalitis is an inflammation of the brain. This neurological disease begins with flulike symptoms. Convulsions may occur and brain damage is also possible. The disease may also cause spinal cord damage, which may lead to motor and sensory problems, and bladder paralysis. Life-threatening complications include respiratory interference, paralysis of the larynx, heart problems, and swelling of the brain.

Of eleven viruses that cause encephalitis and eight that occasionally cause it, seven are transmitted by tick bites. These include Russian encephalitis (or tick-borne encephalitis, TBE), louping ill, powassan, hemorrhagic fever, Kyasanur Forest disease (KFD), Omsk fever, and Crimean fever.

Misdiagnosis sometimes occurs because stroke

can be confused with viral encephalitis. Bacterial meningitis and brain abscess can also mimic viral encephalitis.

TICK-BORNE ENCEPHALITIS

TBE occurs in Europe, Russia (in the far-eastern USSR), and in southern Scandinavia. Over 2,000 cases are reported annually. The disease is seasonally related to peak tick populations. The disease usually affects adults over twenty years old and persons in occupations that bring them into contact with ticks. Family outbreaks are the result of drinking contaminated milk from infected cattle.

In Europe, TBE is mild with a mortality rate of 1 to 2 percent. However, in the Far East, it is very severe, with a mortality rate of 25 percent. In the United States, the disease usually occurs in the northeastern states. Louping ill usually causes encephalitis in cattle and sheep in Great Britain. It occasionally occurs in humans who work with these animals. Powassan has occurred only in New England and eastern Canada, with death occurring in half the few cases that have been documented.

Human beings also can be accidentally infected as a result of contact with rodents, ground-dwelling birds, goats, sheep, cattle, dogs, and cats. Transmission can also occur through drinking unpasteurized sheep or goat milk or eating their cheeses.

SIGNS AND SYMPTOMS. TBE in Europe begins seven to fourteen days after the bite, with flulike symptoms, followed by a period of remission for several days, and then the abrupt onset of encephalitis symptoms.

TBE in the Far East begins with fever, headache, and stomach problems. This is followed by depressed senses, coma, convulsions, and paralysis. In some cases, the rash associated with Lyme disease occurs.

Louping ill resembles European TBE. Fever followed by the development of encephalitis symptoms, which are usually severe, indicates Powassan. Some slight paralysis may occur.

Diagnosis is made by isolating the virus from brain tissue or, in TBE, from blood in the early phase of the illness.

PREVENTION. A TBE vaccine is available in Eastern Europe and the USSR for people who work in forestry, agriculture, and the military. Protective clothing, repellents, insecticides, and rodent control, along with Lyme disease precautions, are the only controls applicable to limit infection.

8 Pest Control

People can come into contact with fleas and ticks at any time of the year. While the insects are normally dormant in the winter, a long warm spell such as is common in the southern areas of the United States, can bring them back into action. No matter where you live, it is important to take year-round precautions.

In the fall, it is a good idea to apply an environmentally safe granular insecticide to the lawn of your home and to fumigate the inside to kill off any pests that are hidden in your carpets and furniture, along with their eggs. Pests love to scurry inside when the weather turns brisk. Then, in the winter, flea infestations can again become common, because as soon as the heat is turned on, the eggs begin to hatch.

The first frost should take care of the pests outside that normally attack pets and hitch a free ride into the house, and as long as the temperature remains below 40° F, these pests will remain dormant.

To keep pets safe from fleas and ticks, they should be cleaned regularly with flea-and-tick shampoos all year around. During the winter, your pets should be bathed indoors and sprayed with flea-and-tick spray. Flea-and-tick collars are only a secondary measure, but it is highly recommended that they be used on a regular basis.

In mid-March, begin your applications of insecticide again, unless there is still snow on the ground. If there are heavy rains expected, or if they are expected in late winter, as is common in the South, wait for drier weather before applying insecticides. Generous amounts of environmentally safe insecticides used outside your home on the lawn and in the garden in the spring will minimize the need for their heavy use in the summer, which is the peak season for fleas and ticks.

Rodent control is also important during the winter, both in the country and in the city. In urban areas it is vital. This population control is of particular importance if you have pets. Rodents will come into your home in search of food, and the first attraction for them is your pet's food, conveniently served at ground level and often left out. If you feed your pets dry food, it is a good idea to transfer the food from its bag to an airtight container for storage. Paper food bags are not protected against sharp rodent teeth. These precautions are particularly vital in areas where Rocky Mountain spotted fever and Lyme disease are common.

In the West, burrowing rodents such as prairie dogs, groundhogs, and squirrels are the hosts of bubonic plague-infected fleas. Extra precautions are needed to protect you and your home from these dangerous pests.

During the summer, keep up the use of insecticides on a regular basis, particularly after heavy rainfall has washed away part of your protection. This regular schedule of treating your house, lawn, and garden every two months or so should be made a habit. If you live near a forest, use insecticides even more frequently—experts recommend applying them every six weeks. It is also recommended that you shampoo your pets every week, use sprays twice a week, and use a reliable flea-and-tick collar.

The substance that is most highly recommended in insecticides, flea-and-tick sprays, and flea-and-tick collars is *pyrethrins*. This substance is the only truly effective killer of ticks and fleas that is currently available. Ultrasonic and so-called "natural" products are not recommended, and may not provide the degree of protection needed to shield your home from these pests, and thus protect your family against infection and disease.

Keep carpets and upholstery clean. Your pets deserve the same treatment; their bedding and the areas that they frequent should also be kept sprayed and clean.

In endemic areas, liberal use of environmentally safe insecticides and pet protection products will provide more than adequate safeguards against ticks, but it is equally important to guard against fleas. Summer—flea and tick season—is the crucial time of year to take precautions, but, precautions and forethought demand that protective and preventive measures be taken all year around.

Your precautions will depend a lot on where you live. If you live, for instance, in a Rocky Mountain spotted fever and/or Lyme disease state, and particularly if you live near a wooded area, you may want to develop your own prevention plan with additional safeguards built into it to protect yourself, your family, and your pets.

Appendix One: Questions and Answers About Lyme Disease

1. What is Lyme disease?

    Lyme disease is a bacterial infection caused by a spiral-shaped microorganism called a spirochete. The name of the Lyme-disease bacterium is *Borrelia burgdorferi*; consequently, the disease often is called Lyme borreliosis.

2. How is Lyme disease spread?

    Lyme disease is spread by the bites of certain ticks. The deer tick, *Ixodes dammini*, is responsible for transmitting the infection in the northeastern and central United States. On the Pacific coast and in the southeast, Lyme disease is spread by black-legged ticks that closely resemble the deer tick.

3. How do ticks carrying Lyme disease differ from other ticks?

    The most important distinction is size. The vector ticks of Lyme disease are much smaller than dog ticks and cattle ticks. The nymph ticks of *Ixodes dammini*, which are chiefly responsible for transmitting infections to humans, are black and no larger than a pinhead. The adult ticks, which may transmit infections in the fall, are only slightly larger.

4. What are the early symptoms of Lyme disease?

The earliest signs of Lyme disease are flulike symptoms (fatigue, chills, fever, headache, muscle and joint pains) and a very characteristic skin rash called erythema migrans. This rash generally appears as a red circular patch that expands slowly, often to a very large size. The center of the patch may clear as the rash enlarges, resulting in a ringlike appearance. The rash may be warm but is not painful.

5. What are the later manifestations of Lyme disease?

Some of the second-stage symptoms of Lyme disease may not appear until weeks or months after the initial onset of the illness. The infection may inflame the heart, leading to disturbances of the heart rhythm. Lyme disease may affect the nervous system, causing muscle weakness or pain and numbness in the face and limbs. Meningitis, an inflammation of the covering of the brain, may occur, resulting in a stiff neck and a severe headache. In later stages of the disease, arthritis may develop and cause the joints to become red, swollen, and painful.

6. How is Lyme disease diagnosed?

Lyme disease is diagnosed from its clinical features and by means of blood tests. Often the blood test does not become positive until several weeks after the onset of illness.

7. Can Lyme disease be treated and cured?

Most Lyme disease patients treated in the early stages of the disease, when only a rash and flulike symptoms are present, will respond favorably to therapy and remain well. Even among patients not treated until the later stages of the disease, the majority respond to therapy. In a small proportion of cases, symptoms may recur, and additional courses of antibiotics are necessary. Permanent damage to joints occurs in a small number of patients.

8. What antibiotics are used to treat Lyme disease?

Tetracyclines (tetracycline, doxycycline) and penicillins (penicillin, ampicillin) are usually used in treating the early stages of Lyme disease. Intravenous penicillin and ceftriaxone are commonly used to treat patients in the later stages of the disease. Other antibiotics and drug combinations are under evaluation.

9. Are there special problems if Lyme disease occurs during pregnancy?

Lyme disease acquired in pregnancy may lead to infection of the fetus. Although some cases of fetal infection resulting in malformations and miscarriage have been reported in untreated cases, there have been no reported instances of an adverse outcome when the pregnant woman was adequately treated.

10. Where does Lyme disease occur?

Lyme disease occurs in a nearly worldwide distribution in North America, Europe, Asia, and Australia. In the United States, Lyme disease has occurred in forty-six states; only Alaska, Hawaii, Montana, Wyoming, Nebraska, New Mexico, and Arizona have not yet reported cases. However, the risk of Lyme disease is greatest in three areas: (1) in the mid-Atlantic and New England states, from Washington, D.C., to Boston; (2) in the upper mid-West in Wisconsin and Minnesota; and (3) on the Pacific coast, especially northern California. Over 90 percent of the nation's cases occur in these three areas.

11. Is Lyme disease spreading?

Yes, the tick vector of Lyme disease is now present in areas of the country where it had not been recognized previously. The tick can be spread by birds, deer, and by humans transporting pets, including horses.

12. Where am I likely to be exposed to ticks carrying Lyme disease?

Ticks prefer wooded areas and overgrown fields. However, in many suburban areas where residential lawns and parks are located within or near woods, ticks may be found in the grass. Local health departments and park or extension services may have information on the local distribution of ticks.

Appendix Two: Ridding Yourself of Pests

Say one summer night you're sitting on the family sofa watching your favorite show on television. All of a sudden you feel an itch. You reach down to scratch the itch. You look around and your family is scratching and so is your pet. You probably have a flea problem.

 ، Don't panic and call an exterminator unless you can see multitudes of fleas hopping all over you, your family, your furniture and carpet, and your pets. There are lots of insecticides on the market that say they combat fleas, but many of them are not very effective. Many are broad spectrum insecticides that are designed to control many kinds of bugs, from roaches to fleas to beetles. You will need an insecticide that is specific for fleas. It should be applicable to killing ticks as well, because if fleas are around, surely ticks will be, too.

You will want a nonstaining insecticide that can be used on many varieties of household surfaces where fleas live and breed. The insecticide should be applicable to carpets, rugs, upholstery, bedding, and pet bedding. The best brands kill adult and pre-adult fleas as well as ticks. They should also contain an insect growth regulator, which is a synthetic hormone that prevents hatching eggs from maturing into adult fleas.

You will need to spray rugs, carpets, draperies, upholstered furniture, pet bedding, and other household areas that your pets frequent. It is important to vacuum an hour or two after you have sprayed in order to remove the dead and stunned bugs, along with their eggs. It is also effective to sprinkle some insecticide powder on the floor and vacuum it into the bag before you begin cleaning. You must remember to throw away disposable vacuum cleaner bags immediately after vacuuming. If your bag is reusable, you will need to wash it and spray it with insecticide before putting it back in the vacuum.

If your pet is over six weeks old, spray with flea-and-tick spray in a well-ventilated area after bathing with a flea-and-tick shampoo. There are multipurpose flea-and-tick specific insecticides that can be used on your pets. Check with your veterinarian about insecticides and sprays. Your vet will also be helpful in advising on how to rid your home and pets of this pest invasion. Be sure to spray from head to toe. Repellents for pets are of little use.

Once pests invade your home, you have to destroy all four stages—egg, larva, pupa, and adult. With ticks, you will usually only be confronted with nymphs and adults. These cycles begin in your home when pets or humans carry these adult pests inside. At this point, the adult female flea finds a host to feed on for the blood necessary to reproduce. Two days later, she lays her eggs, and within one to twelve days, the eggs hatch into larvae. These larvae then feed, and after seven to twenty-four days they spin cocoons and hide in your carpets, bedding, and upholstered furniture. These pupae can hide for up to a year, or until warmth or body

101

pressure signals the presence of a food source—namely you or those you love.

You have to treat your yard in order to prevent outside infestation from coming inside. Your veterinarian can also give advice about this.

The most important thing is to establish a regular routine to eliminate pests and to keep them away.

1. Initially, fumigate your home.
2. Vacuum to remove eggs, pupae, and adults along with larvae of the pests.
3. Treat your pets.
4. Treat your yard.
5. Make it a routine and keep it a routine to treat your home, yard, and pets.
6. Cleanliness is essential.
   • Shampoo pets regularly
   • Launder pet bedding
   • Spray and vacuum regularly
   • Keep corners, crevices, and closets clean of lint, pet hair, and dust. This will deprive pests of their adopted homes.

All of the above will help you to control ticks and will minimize the risk of lice infestation.

If you are returning from an outing in local parks or forests, especially in an endemic area, check for ticks on yourself and on your clothing.

When you are going on vacation, take along plenty of insecticide and repellent, and spray the inside of your car.

FOR LICE INFESTATIONS

With a louse infestation, you will have to eliminate eggs, nymphs, and adults.

Lice can invade the cleanest of homes, but strict cleanliness will minimize the risk of infestation. If your home is invaded:

1. Call your physician immediately.
2. Check all family members for head lice and treat the whole family with the appropriate treatment as recommended by your doctor.
3. Keep your hair brushed and combed.
4. Clean all clothes and bedding. Wash in very hot water, iron seams, and iron pillowcases.
5. Fumigate your house if necessary.
6. If a child comes home with head lice, notify school authorities immediately. Don't wait for someone else to do it. Other children may become infested while you wait, and the problem will spread.

If you contact crab lice or body lice, see your doctor immediately for treatment. With cases of crab lice, it is important to be checked for venereal disease.

Glossary

Agent—a substance or thing that causes a reaction.

Anterior—referring to the front.

Antibodies—a protein made by lymph tissue that defends against bacteria, viruses, or other foreign bodies.

Antimicrobes—a substance that kills microorganisms such as bacteria.

Aspiration pneumonia—a form of pneumonia caused by breathing in vomit or a foreign substance.

Atherosclerosis—a common disorder of the arteries in which plaque builds up on artery walls, making them thick and hardened, thus lessening circulation.

Bacterium—the singular of *bacteria*.

Botulism—an often fatal form of food poisoning.

Cerebrospinal fluid—the fluid that flows through and protects the brain and spinal cord.

Coagulate—to clot, congeal, or thicken into a mass.

Concomitant—accompanying.

Cultures—the product of the growth of microorganisms or tissues for scientific study.

Distention—the state of being expanded or swollen.

Endemic—a disease or infection common to a geographic area or population.

Exacerbation—an increase in the seriousness of a disease; greater intensity of symptoms.

Guillain-Barré Syndrome—a disorder involving inflammation of many nerves; it is linked to a viral infection or with immunization, sometimes causing paralysis.

Hepatitis—inflammation of the liver.

Host—a plant or animal that provides food for a parasite.

Larvae—plural of larva; the immature, wingless feeding stage of an insect.

Malaise—a feeling of lack of health or of not being well, usually indicative of or accompanying the onset of disease.

Molt—to shed skin or feathers that will be followed by new growth.

Neurological—associated with the study of nerves and the nervous system.

Nymph—the young of an insect that undergoes incomplete (or simple) metamorphosis.

Nonspecific—not specific to, or not caused by specific disease organism.

Palpitations—rapid heartbeats.

Pandemic—a disease that occurs in large populations: i.e., influenza.

Papule—a small, solid, raised pimple-like bump on the skin.

Parasite—an organism that lives or feeds on another

Pathogen—any microorganism capable of causing disease.

Pathogenic—capable of producing a disease.

Prostrate—extend into a flat, horizontal position.

Protean—assuming different forms.

Renal failure—kidney failure.

Self-limited—limited by its own nature; having a definite course.

Shunt—to divert from one part to another (as in a surgical passage to *shunt* blood).

Sputum—material coughed up from lungs and spit out of the mouth. Sometimes contains blood or pus.

Steppe—one of the vast and usually treeless plains in southeastern Europe or Asia.

Syphilis—a sexually transmitted disease that causes extensive damage to the body.

Terated—deformed.

Vector—an organism that transmits a pathogen.

Vertigo—dizziness.

Virulence—the quality or strength of sickness or malignancy.

Viscid—having a thick, sticky consistency; viscous.

For Further Reading

Bailey, Eva. *Disease and Discovery*. New York: David & Charles, 1985.

Durie, Bruce. *Medicine*. Morristown, New Jersey: Silver Burdett, 1987.

Garrell, Dale C., and Solomon Snyder. *Medical Diagnosis*. New York: Chelsea House, 1989.

Garrell, Dale C., and Solomon Snyder. *Public Health*. New York: Chelsea House, 1989.

Landau, Elaine. *Lyme Disease*. New York: Franklin Watts, 1990.

Turner, Derek. *The Black Death*. White Plains, New York: Longman, 1978.

Zinsser, Hans. *Rats, Lice and History*. Boston: Little Brown, 1984.

Index

Jarisch-Herxheimer
reaction, 46, 73
Johnson, Russell C., 18

Kyasanur Forest disease
(KFD), 90

Letopsyllus fleas, 26
Lice, 9, 10, 26–27, 66,
69–72, 77, 102–103
Louping ill, 90–92
Louse-borne relapsing
fever, 26, 70–74
Lyme disease, 9, 10, 70
cases of, 11–13, 34–
38
cause of, 11, 17–19,
27–28, 33
detection and
diagnosis of, 44,
46–47
endemic areas for,
20, 58
prevention
precautions, 54,
56–60, 94
questions and
answers about,
96–99
signs and symptoms
of, 14, 15, 33–47,
49, 51–52
tests for, 44, 46
three stages of, 40,
42–44
treatment of, 35–37,
46–52, 54

Mice, 18, 28, 32, 54, 55,
63
Milk, 82, 83, 91
Murine typhus, 79–80

Neurological
complications, 43, 74–
75
Nosopsyllus fleas, 25

Omsk fever, 90
Ornithodoros ticks, 70,
74

Paralysis, 38, 42, 52
Penicillin, 18, 19, 46, 49,
75
Pentamidine, 90
Permanone, 56
Permethrin, 63
Pest control, 93–95,
100–103
Pets, 9, 30, 59, 73, 93–
95, 101
Plagues, 64–65, 67, 83–
86
Pneumonic plague, 83,
85
Possums, 30
Powassan, 90–92
Pulex fleas, 25
Pyrethans, 95

Q fever, 70, 82–83

Rabbits, 28, 30
Rats, 65, 66

Repellents, 56, 59, 75, 80, 85, 90, 92, 101, 102

Rickettsia bacteria, 69

Rickettsia prowazekii bacteria, 77

Rickettsia ricketsii bacteria, 80

Rocky Mountain spotted fever, 17, 20, 70, 80–82, 94

Rodents, 26, 30, 71, 74, 75, 79, 80, 84, 88, 91, 94

Sheep, 26, 30, 82, 83, 91

Spielman, Andrew, 15

Spilopsyllus fleas, 25–26

Spirochetes, 11, 17–19, 22, 28, 33, 40, 44–46, 48, 54, 60, 70

Squirrels, 94

Steere, Allen C., 12–13, 15, 19

Tetracycline, 46, 48–49, 75, 83

Tick-borne encephalitis (TBE), 90–92

Tick-borne relapsing fever, 73–75

Tick paralysis, 70, 75–76

Ticks, 9–11, 13, 15–28, 30–33, 36, 49, 54, 63, 64, 66, 67, 69–70, 80, 82, 88–91, 93–95, 100–102
 removal of, 60

Trench fever, 26

Trepnema palladum bacteria, 46

Typhus, 19, 26, 66, 68–69, 71, 77–80

Versinia pestis bacteria, 83

Viral encephalitis, 90–91

Wood ticks, 76, 81, 86

World Health Organization, 84

Xenopsyllus fleas, 26

About the Author

Sean Mactire is a research intelligence analyst involved in the field of public health. His studies have been concerned with mental health issues, family wellness, and child safety/protection. Mr. Mactire is currently working on a book about head injury. He was the designer of a public health disease-prevention campaign called "Project Family Safeguard." This campaign was endorsed by the U.S. Public Health Service and promoted by RKO Radio.

Mr. Mactire is continuing his research work, which includes a comprehensive study of violence. He lives in Oklahoma City.

cl

CARDS